Sales Reps *are* Free

The CEO's Guide to Hypergrowth

Bill Conifer

Dedicated to those talented, individuals that drive commerce
for the betterment of humanity:
Founders, CEOs, VCs, Professors,
and especially Sales Reps.

New business, new technologies, and new capital sources have reduced poverty for one billion people in the past 20 years.

—Economist June 1, 2013

Sales Reps Are Free – Bill Conifer – 1st Edition 2014

ISBN-13: 978-1505405033

TABLE OF CONTENTS

INTRODUCTION

Why CEOs Need to Read This Book

This book is written for CEOs.

These principles of hypergrowth are not taught in business schools or executive programs. They are the result of 30+ years of the author observing, starting companies, building companies, funding companies, sitting on Boards, being the CEOs, plus selling, and sales management and advising, mostly in Silicon Valley. Once developed, these Principles were tested with four in-depth research projects across four different product and service companies. The results of those projects were phenomenal. Two of the companies went public within one year of completion of our project, two other's growth went from 10% to over 50%.

In this book you will learn:

1. The job of the sales rep (hint: it's not to sell),

2. The math behind why sales reps are free,

3. How to reliably get new customers,

4. How to develop motivational sales compensation plans,

5. How to manage sales reps, and

6. How to convert your company into a sales-centric growth machine.

You'll also learn why mature sales reps don't and shouldn't bring in new customers; you will understand the Sales-Curve, and why your current compensation plan drives your best sales reps out of your company.

If you agree with our Principles, you'll want to have all your VPs read the book as well. Then implement these principles, wait three to six months, and watch your revenue growth take off.

We will put updates and, hopefully, put your hypergrowth sales stories on our website www.SalesRepsAreFree.com. To stay up to date, follow us on Twitter (@SalesRepsAreFree), and Facebook (www.facebook.com/SalesRepsAreFree).

Feel free to make any and all suggestions to bill@salesrepsarefree.com. We are still learning.

Bill Conifer

Bill Conifer

bill@salesrepsarefree.com

SECTION 1

THE "SALES REPS ARE FREE" PHILOSOPHY

CHAPTER ONE

Sales Reps Don't Sell

Back when I was selling computers for Minicomputer Corp. and a $100,000 order was big, there was an $8 million opportunity ($40+ million in 2013 dollars) at Aero Corp. They needed 272 computers. It would be the largest order in the history of our company.

I took my Sales VP to visit Aero Corp. three times. I took the CEO in when I had clearly already lost the order. I had Special Systems redesign our terminal. I had the Colorado factory repaint our printers in Aero's colors. Then, in desperation, I had legal threaten to sue them. I was doing everything I could and still losing. Finally, after Aero Corp. had already placed the order with another company, they relented and decided in our favor.

Did I sell that account? Hell no! The CEO, did. The VP of Sales did. The head of Special System did. The Maine factory manager did. I hate to say it, but the lawyer did. All I did was bring those resources to bear to cause the customer to order.

I like to ask CEOs an obvious question: "What is the job of a sales rep?" Yes, I am irritating, but CEOs, having good social skills, indulge me and answer, "To sell." They typically don't say what they're actually thinking which is, "To sell, stupid."

I contend that if you think the job of a sales rep is to sell, you will always be frustrated because you won't think they're doing their job. Perhaps these sentiments sound familiar.

> "Joe didn't really sell it; the VP of Engineering did."

> "That order came in from the trade show. Sales had nothing to do with it."

> "It was the custom tooling that sold that order."

While woefully common, such sentiments are wrong. Sales reps don't sell. That's not their job. **The job of a sales rep is to bring those resources to bear to cause the customer to order.** If you—and your company—believe this, you will love your sales force, support them, and happily pay their commissions in full. You'll even modify many of your company policies to help the selling process.

Now, when your rep brings the VP of Engineering along to close an order, he's doing his job. When he asks you, the CEO, to make a sales call, you go. It's the rep's job to do what is necessary to get the order, and it's the company's job to support him.

Minicomputer Corp. could have easily not paid my $252,000 commission (about $1,260,000 in 2013 dollars) for the Aero Corp. order. The customer had moved the program to Washington DC, well outside my Palo Alto territory. We had to give a 62%

discount just to win the order, meaning we probably lost money on the deal. And I didn't even sell it. I only brought resources to bear. Minicomputer Corp. wisely (and thankfully) understood I had done my job, and they paid the commission.

I didn't "sell" Aero Corp. I just brought resources to bear to cause the customer to order. If you view the reps' job this way, your entire attitude toward your sales force will change, and they and your company will experience hypergrowth for your tenure.

CHAPTER 2

Why Sales Reps Really Are Free

I'm sitting in my hotel suite at the Waldorf Astoria in New York with two AsiaSoft executives staring at me. Jenny Toms, from VC Partners, says: "Bill can solve your sales growth problem. Tell them Bill." I'm a deer in headlights. Jenny might as well have said, "Bill's a comedian. Say something funny."

The two executives sit listlessly as I attempt to ask questions. I am getting short answers with no elaboration. Where is Colombo or Monk when I need them? Clearly this is a perfunctory meeting meant only to appease their major investor. The room grows increasingly uncomfortable.

> "How many sales reps?"
> *"Five."*
> "All over the US?"
> *"No."*
> "Where?"
> *"Boston."*
> "On commission?"
> *"Yes."*

And so it continues in a painful, staccato style. Pulling teeth would be more pleasant, at least then you have Novocaine.

I continue to quiz them about their product (software I don't understand), their markets (enterprise users, which I also don't understand), their sales approach (internet lead generation with a demo if the customer asks), and finally, where they want to be in five years (bigger).

I begin to form a hypothesis. Their sales program is anemic and far too small to meet their or their investor's five year goals. I could really help them, but only if they want to be helped. The AsiaSoft executives readily admit the market for their software is bigger in Europe than the US, but when I ask what their sales hiring plans are for Europe, they look at me as if I have two heads and retreat back to one word answers.

They admit the US federal government is placing a lot of orders, especially the military, but they have no plans for a sales office in DC. When I suggest establishing a sales office in Washington DC, they reply, "We don't need an office in DC." Since I already think I will never see them again, I answer cynically, "I agree you don't need a DC office; you need five DC sales offices: one for the Army, one for the Navy, one for the Air Force, one for the Federal Government, and one for commercial users, each with five sales reps."

I want out of the room, luckily, so do they. They stand, say their good-byes, and, at last, the meeting is over. I don't expect to hear from them again.

Six months later they call. Shockingly, they want me to invest and join their Board. They have tested some of my tenets like "Sales reps cause sales" and "If you want to grow your business geometrically, you have to grow your sales force geometrically." It turns out the quiet Chairman not only heard me, he internalized what I was saying, tested the concepts, and then called.

Five years later this tiny software company reported sales growth of over 3000%. The company now has 192 sales reps in 17 offices around the world—Munich, Paris, Hong Kong, Sidney—and business is booming. AsiaSoft has more than doubled revenue each year, typically beating their sales forecast by 20-30%. They are my best students, though back in that hotel, I never would have predicted it.

Why AsiaSoft's Sales Reps Are Free

The reason I was so excited to work with AsiaSoft, and the reason my input was particularly helpful to them, was that their sales numbers were especially strong. Following a month of product training, a new sales rep paid for himself only six weeks after he started selling. Six weeks! That was the fastest I had ever seen. Here are the numbers:

Figure 2.1 Cost of AsiaSoft's New Sales Rep after 2.5 Months	
Base Salary:	$3,000/month
Commission:	6% of Revenue
Ave. Time to Close First Order:	10 Weeks
Revenue from First Order:	$8,000
10-Week Base Cost of Rep:	$7,500
Commission Cost of Rep:	$480
10-Week Total Cost of Rep	$7,980
Net Cost of New Rep:	Free! (Okay, they made us $20)

From six weeks on, AsiaSoft's reps aren't just free; they're highly profitable, usually contributing $250,000+ to the company's gross margin each year thereafter.

Even with 192 reps already on board, this ROI holds true. New phone reps still pay for himself or herself within six weeks and then pays the company $250,000+ per year while making a lot of money for themselves. In fact, one phone rep made over $300,000 in commission on a single sale, but more on that later.

Once you have a great product that's competitively-priced and addresses a large and growing market, then adding sales reps will add revenue, lots of revenue, just as it does for Asia Soft.

How to See If Your Sales Reps Are Free

To see if your reps are free, estimate the revenue you think a new hire rep can generate from the date of hire. It's usually easiest to estimate the number of sales and then multiply by the average price per sale. Remember to be conservative, and also remember it may take three to six months for your new rep to sell anything. Then you can calculate the direct costs associated with your new rep, compare the two and estimate your return on investment.

As an example, here are the estimates and calculations we did for EduSoft, a company making classroom computers for education markets. EduSoft sold systems consisting of 30 computers for $20,000. It was a complex selling environment, involving the individual school, the school district, and the state department of education, which is probably why new reps didn't produce much in their first few months.

Estimated Sales by a New Hire Rep at EduSoft

Figure 2.2 Edusoft New Hire Sales Revenue Forecast													
Month	1	2	3	4	5	6	7	8	9	10	11	12	Total
Units Sold	0	0	0	1	2	1	2	2	3	3	4	4	22
Revenue ($1,000)				$ 20	$ 40	$ 20	$ 40	$ 40	$ 60	$ 60	$ 80	$ 80	$ 440

Costs and Margins for a New Rep at EduSoft

Figure 2.3: EduSoft New Sales Rep Costs and Revenue			
Revenue Assumptions		Costs Assumptions	
Revenue/Sale:	$20,000	Base Salary:	$60,000/year
Margin 50%:	50%	Commission:	3% of Revenue
Margin Dollars/Sale:	$10,000	Office Expense:	$2,000/month
		Benefits:	25%

Now we can put these figures into a standard profit and loss format. See Figure 2.4 on facing page.

Hiring a new rep on January 1st gives EduSoft $440,000 of additional revenue and $104,500 of additional profit. That's money they wouldn't otherwise have, and that's just one hire in their first year. Imagine what would happen if they hired 12.

Figure 2.5 New EduSoft Rep Summary		
Revenue	$	440,000
Margin (50%)	$	220,000
Costs	$	115,500
Profit	$	104,500

The new rep becomes cash positive in month four and breaks even in month eight. By the end of the year, EduSoft's cost of selling is down to 14% of revenue. Sales Reps aren't free; they pay you.

Figure 2.4 First Year Profitability of a New Rep at EduSoft

Month	1	2	3	4	5	6	7	8	9	10	11	12	Total
Sales:													
Units ($20K each)	0	0	0	1	2	1	2	2	3	3	4	4	22
Revenue/mo.				$ 20,000	$ 40,000	$ 20,000	$ 40,000	$ 40,000	$ 60,000	$ 60,000	$ 80,000	$ 80,000	$ 440,000
COGS (50%)*				$ 10,000	$ 20,000	$ 10,000	$ 20,000	$ 20,000	$ 30,000	$ 30,000	$ 40,000	$ 40,000	$ 220,000
Margin				$ 10,000	$ 20,000	$ 10,000	$ 20,000	$ 20,000	$ 30,000	$ 30,000	$ 40,000	$ 40,000	$ 220,000
Expenses:													
Base Salary	$ 5,000	$ 5,000	$ 5,000	$ 5,000	$ 5,000	$ 5,000	$ 5,000	$ 5,000	$ 5,000	$ 5,000	$ 5,000	$ 5,000	$ 60,000
Commission (3%)				$ 600	$ 1,200	$ 600	$ 1,200	$ 1,200	$ 1,800	$ 1,800	$ 2,400	$ 2,400	$ 13,200
Benefits (25%)	$ 1,250	$ 1,250	$ 1,250	$ 1,400	$ 1,550	$ 1,400	$ 1,550	$ 1,550	$ 1,700	$ 1,700	$ 1,850	$ 1,850	$ 18,300
Office Costs ($2K/mo.)	$ 2,000	$ 2,000	$ 2,000	$ 2,000	$ 2,000	$ 2,000	$ 2,000	$ 2,000	$ 2,000	$ 2,000	$ 2,000	$ 2,000	$ 24,000
Total Expenses	$ 8,250	$ 8,250	$ 8,250	$ 9,000	$ 9,750	$ 9,000	$ 9,750	$ 9,750	$ 10,500	$ 10,500	$ 11,250	$ 11,250	$ 115,500
ROI:**													
Profit/mo.	$ (8,250)	$ (8,250)	$ (8,250)	$ 1,000	$ 10,250	$ 1,000	$ 10,250	$ 10,250	$ 19,500	$ 19,500	$ 28,750	$ 28,750	$ 104,500
Cumulative Profit	$ (8,250)	$ (16,500)	$ (24,750)	$ (23,750)	$ (13,500)	$ (12,500)	$ (2,250)	$ 8,000	$ 27,500	$ 47,000	$ 75,750	$ 104,500	

*COGS is "Cost of Goods Sold"   **ROI is "Return on Investment"

Hiring new sales reps may be the best deal in all of business. Why CEOs don't know this is mind boggling, and why business schools don't teach it is even more mind boggling. Maybe they don't know it either.

What Happens When You Hire More Reps

At EduSoft, we strongly recommended they promote three of their best reps to regional sales managers and have each of them hire four reps. The company had just endured two years of stagnant sales growth and was receptive to our suggestions. Our analysis, shown above, actually proved quite conservative. With more reps, EduSoft's revenue skyrocketed. A company with $40 million in revenue and no growth is probably worth only $20 million but soon EduSoft was on a $60 million revenue run rate growing at 50% per year and worth $250 million. They went public nine months after they implemented our recommendations.

I have had more than one CEO tell me, "If only my revenue would go up, I would love to hire more sales reps." I try to avoid telling them what I'm thinking, which is: "Well sir, that's about the dumbest thing I've ever heard."

Remember: Sales reps cause sales, not sales cause sales reps. Hiring reps is how you grow your revenue, not something you do after it has grown. Sure it can be tough to commit to hiring when cash is tight, but your new reps will very soon prove free. And if sales reps are free, then hiring isn't really an expense.

Even "Failing" Reps Were Free

At one AsiaSoft meeting, I noticed the number of sales reps had gone down, a rather stunning development for me. With reps paying for themselves in six weeks, the last thing I expected was fewer of them. When I inquired, the CEO told me, "Those reps weren't working hard and weren't selling up to expectations, so we terminated them." It was understandable, until I looked at the data.

The meeting was in August. Assuming the "failing" reps had continued to sell at their subpar rate for the remaining four months of the year, they still would have added $800,000 to our revenue and $600,000 to our profits. Given our commission plan, and low $3,000 per month base, the non-performing reps were still materially contributing.

At Retail Buying Group., even a failing rep paid for himself in eight months. This blew me away. A "subpar" new rep would bring in one order per month, after five months with no sales at all. A "good" rep, in contrast, was expected to close four new customers per month. When I did the calculations, I realized the failing rep still made Retail Buying Group money.

Retail Buying Group is somewhat unique in that they are a buying service that aggregates purchase orders from over 3,500 retailers. This enables Retail Buying Group to negotiate bigger discounts than the individual stores can on their own. To join, you need to sign a five year contract costing approximately $2,000 per month, saving you up to $5,000 per month on your purchases. Failing reps brought in one new order per month, but that was an annuity order, meaning that each order yielded $2,000 every month thereafter for five years. The reps cost us $8,000 per month. So after four months of "failing", the reps are covering their cost since they now have four accounts paying $2,000 per month or $8,000. By the fifth month they are positive contributors to the business.

The only reason to terminate an incrementally profitable lower-performing rep is to make room for a higher performing rep. You shouldn't terminate a "failing" rep unless your sales managers are maxed out, i.e. already have five reps reporting to them (a concept I'll discuss more in chapter 7). Even then, I'd advise you only to terminate a marginal rep only after you hire the new rep.

Why Hiring Sales Reps Doesn't Guarantee Success

For sales reps to produce sales, and thus be free, you have to have a good company in a good market...well, at least a reasonable company in a reasonable market. It would be naive to hire tons of sales reps if you didn't have a competitive product, an attractive price, and a large and growing market. But, if you do have those things, doubling your number of sales reps will double your sales (next year).

CHAPTER 3

Why You Should Re-Draw Your Organizational Chart

In my first sales job at Rugged Computer Corp., I had the pleasure of working for a brilliant VP of Sales, Bill Rome. One day a consultant asked our upper management staff to draw an organization chart of the company. Bill drew this:

Figure 3.1 The Sales Centric View

In Bill's view, the sales reps were the center of the company and the company only existed to help them sell. (You could draw a chart with the customer in the middle and it would be more accurate, but for our purposes, let's leave the sales reps there.) If the VP of Finance was needed to design a leasing program, so be it. If engineering was needed to educate the customer on an interface design, then call them in. If the CEO had to travel to Japan to secure a partnership, that was fine. To Bill, they all reported to the sales department.

Needless to say, Bill was a very successful VP of Sales and the company was very successful as well. Yes, Rugged Computer Corp. had a great strategy, brilliant engineering, adequate venture funding, and a solid board—all of which, in Bill's opinion, were there to help the sales reps sell.

Was Bill Crazy?

Think about it: the company exists to serve their customers. It's a machine that turns effort into sales, and everything it does is in pursuit of that transaction, in pursuit of the sale. That's why engineers design things. That's why marketers advertise them. That's why people come to work. The sale is the end result of everyone's effort at the company. That's how you serve your customers. Selling should be at the center of your company.

What does this mean in practice? In the previous chapter I discussed how the job of a sales rep is to bring the resources to bear to cause the customer to order. Well, the corollary is: **The job of the company is to supply those resources to their sales reps.** Give them all they need to close the sale.

For example, marketing can help by generating hot leads; engineering can help with better, more exciting products; finance can help by liberalizing credit; and operations can help by shipping today. Everyone, in their own way, should work towards helping your sales reps.

I've carried this sales-centric philosophy with me ever since Bill sketched his diagram. It was a big part of his success at Rugged Computer Corp. and was later the key to the success at over ten companies including three that went public and five that merged successfully.

How to Sell the Cruise Missile Guidance System

Bill walked into our corporate office at Rugged Computer one day and said, "We need to ship all the training computers and peripherals to Missile Systems today."

Mind you, I had 10 customers coming in for training the next day who would need these very computers. So after coming off the ceiling, I let out a collective and pained, "Why?"

"They have to write proof of concept software for a government program they are trying to sell," Bill explained. Of course the reason didn't actually matter, the fact Bill said it needed to be done was sufficient. If Bill said we needed to ship today, we were going to ship today. He cajoled the warehouse to assemble the order immediately. Instead of resisting, our training staff began testing and retesting all the equipment. Operations set up the FedEx delivery for the following day. And when everything was ready, a crack team of sales reps, assistants, engineers, and the CEO himself boxed up the order and loaded it on the FedEx truck.

We ended up selling over 10,000 computers on that program

over the next five years. It turns out they were demonstrating their concept for the guidance system of a new weapon: the Cruise Missile.

I ended up using engineering prototypes for the computer training class. While engineering was screaming at me, the customers loved using new machines months before they were announced.

Her Majesty's Customer Service

Here is a conversation I had with a British customer when I mailed my first computer accessories catalog, Instant Supply, to the UK. As background, I should point out it was difficult to buy anything in the UK in the '80s. The Brits seemed to hate customers interrupting their day. British companies were not sales-centric. At least not back then.

> CUSTOMER (WITH PROPER BRITISH ACCENT): I received your catalog and would like to know how, kind Sir, to establish an account.

> ME: You buy something.

> CUSTOMER: You can't do that. What if I didn't pay?

> ME: Then you couldn't buy my great products or experience my great service ever again.

> CUSTOMER: Sounds reasonable. If I did order, when might you, in the kindness of your heart, be able to ship the order to my London office?

ME: If you order in the next 30 minutes, it will be on your desk at ten tomorrow, unless you need it faster, then I can put it on the Liverpool train and you can pick it up at Euston Station four hours from now.

CUSTOMER: You can't do that.

ME: Try me.

CUSTOMER (NEXT DAY): You did it! Thanks.

I wanted my company to be different; I wanted it to be extremely easy to buy from. Let's look at my corporate policies that made this delightful and profitable exchange possible.

• **Finance:** I gave credit without a credit check. Insane? I don't think so. I think credit checks are generally superfluous and detrimental to sales. This was especially true in Instant Supply's case. We sold computer supplies and accessories to businesses. They had already passed a major credit check when they bought a computer for over $50,000. Our orders were for $300. I happily gave them credit without a credit check, and my bad debt still ran less than 1%, a small price for all the extra sales I received by not delaying shipment for a credit check.

• **Operations:** I had set a policy of same day shipment for orders received before 3:30 PM. I could see no reason, if the product was in stock, why we couldn't get it shipped. This took organization and diligence, and probably increased fulfillment costs, but my sales reps and customers loved it. I can still hear my sales people yelling, "Quigley, another order, its only 3:29." (Michael Quigley was our warehouse manager.)

• **Inventory:** With a same day shipment policy, we had to be in stock. This wasn't always easy. My first UK catalog included a connector that was in preposterously high demand. In desperation, we ordered a six month supply. That sold out before it even arrived, so we tripled our order and managed to keep some in stock.

At Instant Supply, I viewed the entire company as groups that existed to help the sales reps sell. Open credit, same day shipping, and guaranteed inventory were an expression of that philosophy. And they helped us sell a lot more than our stiff-upper-lip competitors.

Try This Test Yourself

If you want to learn about your company's attitude toward helping sales reps, gather your senior management staff and give them this written quiz:

• What can your departments do to help sales reps sell more?

• What can your departments do to make it harder for sales reps to sell?

Here are some common answers to the "make it harder" question:

- Legal: "Complete a 27-page legal document before approving an order."

- Marketing: "Wait four weeks for an exclusive territory map."

- Finance: "Apply for credit with five references."

- Legal: "Sign a complicated software license agreement."

- Finance: "Pre-pay in full."

When we did sales growth consulting, asking these questions was always one of the most enlightening moments. The answers to the "make it harder" question usually resemble most departments' current operating policies. This test will shock you.

As you go through each department, consider changing to policies that save the reps time, make it easier for your customers to purchase, easier to pass credit checks, and faster for the factory to ship or provide the service.

I would argue that when all is said and done, the value of your company is not what it sells but how and to whom it sells it. Your company's value is your channel of distribution, and your customer relationships (I include brand equity under this banner), not your technology. A competitor could reverse engineer your product in 9 or 18 months, but it would take years to recreate your channel of distribution or your motivated sales force. That's the source of your value, and the sales department is building it. So structure your entire company to support them fully.

CHAPTER 4

How to Get More Selling Time

The best way to get more selling time is to practice customer excuse deprivation: "Take away any excuse for your customers not to buy from your company today."

Most internet companies have this down cold. Look at Amazon: same day shipment, great guarantee, ship from a warehouse near you, and great prices. Why not buy from Amazon? And, you don't need to talk to anybody to get this great service. Is your company as easy?

Have you ever tried buying a $2 battery at Radio Shack? They want your name, address, and first born child before you can buy with cash.

At Retail Buying Group, it took them three weeks and several calls to map an exclusive territory for a new reseller, an important, but straightforward task that actually took four hours. That was three weeks during which the customer could have easily moved on; certainly, we weren't demonstrating our superior customer service.

Companies excel at making sales more difficult, putting encumbrances in their potential customer's way and burdening their own sales reps with non-selling tasks. I suggest you remove, or at the very least mitigate, these encumbrances. Make it easy for your prospects to say "yes", and for your reps to focus on eliciting that "yes".

Corporate Sanity Check

Perhaps you're thinking: "We already do that." Ok, then try this exercise. List, department by department, all the tasks your company has piled onto the selling process or sales reps. Here are some common examples.

- Legal: "We need this 29 page reseller agreement and NDA signed before we can process their order."

- Finance: "We need prepayment or a letter of credit, or a credit application with financials and two bank references. We don't know who this company is!"

- Manufacturing: "It wasn't in the forecast, so we won't build it." Or: "Yes, it was in the forecast but the sales department always lies, so I didn't buy the parts."

- Marketing: "We need the sales reps to fly in early to set up the display for the trade show."

- Customer Support: "The sales reps should handle the installation and customer training. It would be good for them."

- VP of Sales: "I want call reports and all the entries in Salesforce [CRM] up to date. I don't care how long it takes."

If You Fail this Test, You Can Fix It

Ask Legal, "What if I limited you to one page on the back of our order acknowledgment for terms, how would you protect me?"

Ask Finance, "If I gave you 24 hours to prove this potential customer is not credit worthy or we will ship, what would be my bad debt loss?"

Ask Manufacturing, "If I want to ship the next day, what would have to change?"

It's natural for other departments to try to erect sales obstacles. It makes their jobs easier, absolves them of any risk, and if sales suffer, well that's not their department's problem. So the obstacles pile on, and the sales rep's job gets harder while everyone else's gets easier. Typically there's no counterbalance in this process. Who can challenge legal? Or finance? Or the factory? Your reps are outgunned. You, as CEO, need to protect them. Hopefully, the VP of Sales is too busy selling.

Trust Should Flow from You to Your Customers

Most companies, especially the finance and legal departments of most companies, believe the opposite. They act like the customer has to prove their worthiness before they can be allowed to purchase. Finance would prefer prepayment so they never have to call a customer to collect. Legal would prefer no transactions, ever. That's their ultimate protection. Zero sales means no bad debt losses and no lawsuits...unfortunately, it also means zero sales. Instead, I suggest trusting your customers, accepting some bad debt risk, and selling more.

Are credit checks the best way to start a customer relationship? Do you even need them? For starters, giving or not giving credit is too important of a selling variable to be left up to the finance department. Credit checks should be your call, and most likely, you don't need them. In my experience, people buy things expecting to pay, especially with business purchases where it's not their own money. Also, the customer will likely need continuing service, parts, etc., and want to maintain good relations with you.

Further, I'm not convinced credit checks even work. Typically when a company goes broke, they go broke fast. They've paid their debts until that point. At Instant Supply, we once did retroactive credit checks on some of our known bad debtors. We checked their credit score three months back when we sold to them. They all passed. They had only recently become insolvent and weren't failing the checks three months prior. To set up credit checks would have cost us $20,000 per month in fees to a credit service and would have delayed shipping by one to three days.

So we didn't have credit checks at Instant Supply. And what did this do to our bad credit loss? It never exceeded 1%. I actually tried, unsuccessfully, to get it higher. My philosophy is that if your bad credit loss is less than 2%, then your credit policies are unnecessarily restricting sales. I advise finance departments to keep liberalizing their policies until bad debt reaches toward 2%.

Your finance and legal departments will miss the forest for the trees. Once, AeroCorp put the US Navy on credit hold. Could anything be stupider? It's much better to start your customer relationships with a sale than with a credit check, NDA, or 29-page contract. I prefer to trust my customers so they will feel comfortable buying from me.

Selling Time is One of Your Company's Most Valuable Resources

Let your reps focus on selling. This is, of course, a corollary to removing the policies that impede sales. Every minute your rep spends chasing down credit apps or filling out account applications, is time she's not selling. But beyond those policies, consider the rep's internal workload.

What non-sales tasks are you making your reps do? Are they spending hours updating the Customer Relationship Manager (CRM) each day? Are they required to precisely track their mileage whenever they leave the office? Do you expect them to log all of their sales calls?

Data entry and database management are corporate tasks. Your sales reps should spend as little time on these as possible. Hire sales assistants to do the work. The added selling time they provide your reps will more than cover the cost. If reps are above a certain rate of sales or quota, exempt them from the CRM system. CRMs can be a nagging time sink.

Sales is the only department expected to fill out call reports and sometimes even send in plans for the coming week. Imagine if you required marketing or finance to fill out a report of what they did last week and what they planned on doing next week, instead of actually doing it. Yet companies do this to sales reps all the time.

One of my great bosses once said, "You can force sales reps to fill out call reports, but you need to motivate them to actually make calls." The calls are far more important.

How Much Revenue is Lost by Corporate Policies?

Stop and think about how much revenue you're losing by corporate policies.

I mentioned how it took Retail Buying Group three weeks to map the territory for a new customer. This was a four hour process, and the rep was not allowed to request the territory map before the sale. So we lost about one month of revenue from each new customer. That was $2,000 across 3,000 customers, or $6,000,000, all for want of same-day territory mapping. And that doesn't even include the customers that cancelled during the three week delay. This is free money.

Similarly, if your rep sells $5 million annually, he is bringing in $2,500 of revenue per hour (assuming a 2000 hour work year). Are you sure you want him setting up your trade show booth?

The best way to evaluate your company's corporate policies is to imagine yourself as a prospective customer, or even call your company and pretend to be one. Are you able to get the attention of a sales rep? Do you have to divulge your address and SAT scores before the rep will give you any information? Are there obstacles in your path to buying, e.g. legal documents, PO formalities, or credit checks? Are they flexible on terms for your specific circumstance? Is the ordering and payment process easy? Can you get your product or service without delay?

Getting these details right will set you apart, since most companies get them wrong.

SECTION 2

KEY SALES-CURVE CONCEPTS

CHAPTER 5

Embracing the S-Curve

At Instant Supply, my catalog company, a new customer would place an average first time order of $70, a second order of $160, and a third of $230. After the third order, customers would continue at the $200 to $300 rate every month for three years.

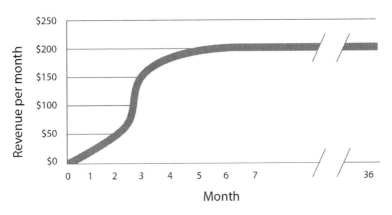

Figure 5.1 Instant Supply New Customer Curve

At EduSoft, a school district would first buy one or two $200 units to evaluate. Then they'd buy a $20,000 classroom system with 30 units and an overnight charging rack. Next came multiple classroom systems, and soon, the entire school district would order several systems per school.

At AsiaSoft a customer would place an $8,000 initial order and over the next three years would usually spend upwards of $100,000 with AsiaSoft.

This is the standard trajectory for new customers. They start with low risk, small dollar purchases and then, as trust builds, move toward bigger and more frequent purchases. On a graph this creates an S-Curve like the one above. Most, if not all, CEOs understand the new customer S-Curve, but what they often don't know is that their new sales reps will follow the same type of S-Curve.

The Sales Rep S-Curve

Just like a new customer, your new sales rep will go through an S-Curve revenue build up. The rep will start slow, then build up sales quickly, and ultimately plateau. This is true even if the rep comes with a "full Rolodex" and previously sold for your main competitor.

Years ago at Minicomputer Corp., a new rep, even one we hired from a competitor like Data General, DEC or HP, would sell at about this pace:

Figure 5.2 Minicomputer New Rep Sales Curve				
Year	1	2	3	4
Revenue	$ 200,000	$ 1,500,000	$ 3,000,000	$ 3,000,000

Or shown another way:

Figure 5.3 Minicomputer Corp's New Rep S-Curve

Similarly, AsiaSoft's telesales reps typically sell nothing for the first six weeks, then one system the next month, two the third, and eventually top out at six systems per month, about $40,000, per month. For the sake of driving the point home, here's what that looks like.

Figure 5.4 AsiaSoft's New Rep S-Curve

AsiaSoft's phone reps go through the same sales S-Curve that Minicomputer Corp.'s outside reps did 30 years ago, albeit more quickly: six months versus three years. Of course AsiaSoft's reps only sell $480K per year compared to Minicomputer Corp.'s $3 million. Different industries and businesses will have different data points, but all new sales reps will follow an S-Curve buildup.

The good news is that once they mature on the S-Curve, your reps will bring in solid revenue month after month. The bad news is that the end of the S-Curve is a plateau, and all sales reps will inevitably hit it. After a certain period, say six months or three years, their revenue simply stops growing. Think about that. Each of your reps are still selling a lot, but your company has no revenue growth. **Unless you keep adding sales reps, your growth will go to zero.**

Why the Sales Rep S-Curve Tops Out

The reason a sales rep tops out is simply time. There are a finite number of sales calls or selling hours in the week. And a mature rep has existing customers who expect his attention, giving him even less time for new customer calls. While he may have a better batting average per call than new reps, the mature rep can't make the day longer. Eventually he is just out of selling time. He can maintain his existing highly productive pace but cannot increase it.

Consider, for example, a rep selling computer systems. He'll need one day in the office for paperwork, setting up leads, filling out call reports, updating Salesforce, servicing past sales, and following up on orders. That leaves enough time for six to eight sales calls per week. If it takes three sales calls to find one qualified potential customer and three calls on that customer to close, he can sell just over one system per week maximum. That's maximum. And that's only if he has no existing customers haranguing him. If the computer systems are $40,000 each, the rep tops out at $2 million in revenue per year (50 weeks * $40,000/ week). There is nothing you, as CEO, can do about this, except add more sales reps and appreciate the $2 million each of your current sales reps are bringing in every year.

"We Need to Make the Sales Reps More Efficient!"

Sales is the only job where CEOs and management consistently move the goal post, believing reps should always do more next year than last year, often a lot more. Imagine an engineer being expected to invent one product this year, two next year, and four the subsequent year. It is equally absurd to expect sales reps to grow their sales every year.

When I ask CEOs how they intend to grow sales without hiring new sales reps, they often answer, "We'll sell more per rep. We need to make the sales reps more efficient!" Okay, with a lot of effort, you may realize a 10% gain, but I've never seen it happen, at least not when the reps are already topped out on the S-Curve.

If your sales reps have topped out, the only way to increase sales is to hire more reps. If you want to double sales, just double your sales force. As we'll see in the next chapter, it works well, but with a slight delay.

CHAPTER 6

Planning Around the S-Curve

"That's next year's problem." VP Sales

There are three critical implications of the sales S-Curve that you should understand and plan around.

1. Consistent sales growth requires consistent sales rep hiring.

2. You can't solve this year's sales problems with this year's sales hires.

3. Annual budgeting crushes sales hiring.

1. Consistent Growth Requires Consistent Hiring.

Let's revisit Minicomputer Corp.'s sales figures from the previous chapter. Each new rep would sell at about this pace:

Figure 6.1 Minicomputer New Rep Sales Curve				
Year	1	2	3	4
Revenue	$ 200,000	$ 1,500,000	$ 3,000,000	$ 3,000,000

Using these numbers as an example, this is what would happen if a start-up company hired five reps over two years, one at the outset and one every six months thereafter.

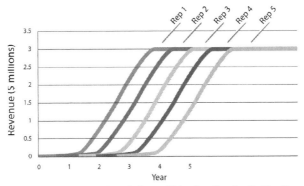

Figure 6.2 New Reps S-Curves Hiring One Rep Per Six Months

This is a good distribution of sales resources. The reps are climbing their S-Curves, and as one plateaus a new one starts taking off. The reps aren't just climbing their own S-Curves though; they are actually creating an S-Curve for the company itself. Look at what they do for overall company revenue (the top-most line).

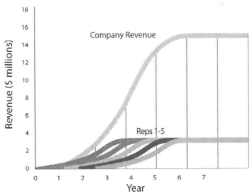

Figure 6.3 Company S-Curve Hiring One Rep Per
Six Months Stopping at Five Reps

The company experiences good growth during the first four years. Its revenue rises as the sum of all five reps climb the S-Curve. It's a great start. But just as each rep will inevitably plateau, so too has the company set itself up to stall. After four and a half years, all the reps have reached the top of their respective S-Curves. All growth stops.

S-Curves are inevitable for sales reps, but you don't want your company to follow one. Reps top out; companies don't need to. To avoid your company topping out, simply hire more reps. Look at what would happen if our example company continued to hire a new rep every six months rather than stopping at five total reps.

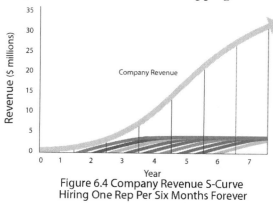

Figure 6.4 Company Revenue S-Curve
Hiring One Rep Per Six Months Forever

Instead of stalling indefinitely at $15 million in revenue, the company maintains consistent growth, hitting $26 million in year six and $31 million the year after. That's more than double what it would have been with five reps. Now, model hiring two reps per month or five reps per month for the next five years and you'll see your company heading toward a $1 billion in revenue.

Your reps, no matter how good, will top out. To keep growing, you have to keep hiring. But...

2. You Can't Solve this Year's Sales Problem with this Year's Sales Hires.

Regardless of their background, it will take time for your new reps to climb the sales S-Curve. Thus, you cannot expect this year's hires to drive much of this year's revenue. Or put another way, to achieve sales growth next year you have to hire reps this year.

Let's consider the new hire sales figures for EduSoft, shown previously. This is a good example of the S-Curve and is helpful here because we can analyze it month by month. Each system, you recall, sold for $20,000 each.

You will certainly see some revenue benefit from hiring a sales rep in January, $440K in this case. But what about hiring a sales rep in July or October? You get the expense this year, but little or no revenue.

Figure 6.5 Edusoft Sales Rep Performance Hired in January												
Month	Jan	Feb	Mar	Apr	May	Jun	Jul	Aug	Sep	Oct	Nov	Dec	Total
Units Sold	0	0	0	1	2	1	2	2	3	3	4	4	22
Revenue ($1,000)				$ 20	$ 40	$ 20	$ 40	$ 40	$ 60	$ 60	$ 80	$ 80	$ 440

A July hire will gross $80K in revenue this year.

Figure 6.6 Edusoft Sales Rep Performance Hired in July						
Month	Jul	Aug	Sep	Oct	Nov	Dec	Total
Units Sold	0	0	0	1	2	1	4
Revenue ($1,000)				$ 20	$ 40	$ 20	$ 80

An October hire will sell nothing.

Figure 6.7 Edusoft Sales Rep Performance Hired in October				
Month	Oct	Nov	Dec	Total
Units Sold	0	0	0	0
Revenue ($1,000)				0

This sales lead time is critical to understand for budgeting cycles. The point is not that you shouldn't hire reps in July or October. The point is that you shouldn't expect those hires to boost this year's revenue. To get growth early this year, you needed to hire last year. To get growth next year, you need to hire now. By next year it's too late.

Here's the good news though: once you endure the zero sales lead time of a new rep, your revenue will continue to climb. Using the same EduSoft figures, if you hired one rep each month in the first year, those 12 reps would collectively sell $9.8 million in the second year. Sure, they would start slow, selling only 87 incremental new customers in year one, but year two would see 489 new customers sold. That is a phenomenal return on the investment you made in year one, and the revenue growth rate will continue for each successive year.

In light of the sales S-Curve, you should hire reps continuously well in advance. And budget accordingly, because...

3. Annual Budgeting Crushes Sales Growth.

Sales reps hired this year are an investment in next year's growth. In that sense, the two years are mutually dependent. Yet with annual budgeting, most companies treat them as independent. They produce a budget that simply meets this year's targets, rather than one that meets this year's targets and invests in next year's sales growth. Such myopic annual budgeting will crush your sales growth in the first half of next year.

Given the S-Curve, reps hired in Q1 will generally pay for themselves this year, but reps hired in Q3 or Q4 will not. Annual budgeting thus discourages any sales rep hiring in the second half of the year. Why would a sales manager or VP spend money this year for a rep that won't pay off until next year? They typically won't. And thus the annual budgeting crushes growth by discouraging investment in future sales.

This concept is easy to see for a catalog company like Instant Supply. The sales curve for an Instant Supply catalog, which for these purposes we can think of as a paper sales rep, was spread over 12 weeks after mailing with few or no sales occurring in the first two to four weeks. We expensed the catalog and postage costs soon after mailing. This accounting killed catalog mailings in the last two months of the fiscal year because we would incur the costs but not realize the revenue until the following year. As a result our sales growth was perennially down in January and February. Going to an 18-month budget fixed this problem.

There's a big difference between creating a budget that works for one year versus creating one that works this year and invests in growth for next year. I would, at a minimum, recommend an 18 month budget so you get visibility into the first half of next year.

Accurately forecasting that revenue is easy: multiply the number of rookie sales reps by the expected S-Curve performance of a rookie, plus the number of mature sales reps by their expected mature S-Curve performance. It is the most accurate revenue forecasting tool I know.

CHAPTER 7

The Rule of Five

VC Capital, a Silicon Valley VC firm, invested in a company whose CEO loved to brag about how many VARs they had signed up. VAR (or Value Added Reseller) is Silicon Valley jargon for an independent sales firm that sells technology to customers in its local territory. They're B-to-B resellers, and this company had signed with 203 of them, much to the CEO's delight. It did sound impressive, until I asked how many sales managers they had managing those 203 VARs. "Four," said the CEO. Four managers for 203 sales firms? I did some quick arithmetic and hazarded the following, "Then you have 20 to 24 VARs that are actually generating revenue." They checked; it was 21.

Was my 20 to 24 a lucky guess? Not at all. The span of control in any complex managerial job is four to six direct reports. Selling technology is certainly a complex job and, therefore, a sales manager can only effectively manage four to six sales reps—five is ideal. With only four managers, I knew this company could only effectively manage 20, maybe 24 sales firms. They could keep signing up new VARs by the dozens, but without enough managers to support and motivate them, those VARs would produce no revenue. The company should have had 40 managers for its 203 VARs.

I call this the Rule of Five. You need one sales manager for every five reps (or VARs or sales rep firms). You can't break this rule and expect it to work. The sixth rep under a manager will likely fail. Count your sales managers; multiply by five, and you have your maximum number of productive sales reps.

Five Isn't Quitting Time

The problem I see over and over in Silicon Valley startups is that companies hire a VP Sales, who hires five sales reps, and then stops. Sales climb the S-Curve for two years and then they hit the growth wall in year three.

Now whenever I'm asked to help a company with strong products in a large and growing market, but with stalled growth, I start by asking the CEO, "How many sales reps do you have?" "Five" is always the answer.

Five was the answer at EduSoft, with $40 million in revenue selling educational computers. It was the answer at AsiaSoft, with $4 million selling enterprise software enhancements. It was the answer at Rugged Computer Corp., with $10 million in revenue selling computers. It was the answer at a $40 million cooperative buying group company and recently it was the answer at a $450 million revenue healthcare company.

It's understandable why this is so common. Five is the number of reps that one VP of Sales can successfully manage. Think about the company's development. First, you hire a VP of Sales.

He starts selling well, but the travel is monopolizing his time. So he hires an East Coast Rep, then one in Chicago, and so on until he gets to five sales reps. He stops there, having hit his managerial limit. Your selling power has gone up 500% (from one to five), and growth appears excellent. It's 600%.

I'll use Minicomputer Corp.'s old sales per rep figures again to demonstrate this growth.

Figure 7.1 Minicomputer New Rep Sales Curve				
Year	1	2	3	4
Revenue	$ 200,000	$ 1,500,000	$ 3,000,000	$ 3,000,000

So your five new reps will generate $1 million for the company in year one, $7.5 million in year two, and $15 million in year three. That's a 1500% growth rate from years one to three. This company is "hot".

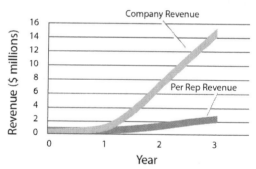

Figure 7.2 Three Year Company Revenue
with five Reps hired initially.

Unfortunately, the growth will soon stop, because having only five reps is as damaging as it is pervasive. By year three, the five reps top out on the S-Curve. They're still doing a great job, selling

$3 million each, but that's all they can humanly do. Revenue flattens indefinitely. VPs start getting fired, first marketing for not generating better leads, then engineering for not inventing more salable products. The venture capitalist calls. The rent is due. General panic sets in.

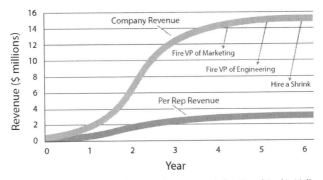

Figure 7.3 Five Year Company Revenue with five Reps hired initially

This is shockingly common in the Silicon Valley. Many otherwise extremely successful startups hit a wall at around $20 to $30 million in revenue specifically because they're stuck at five reps, each of whom are maxed at about $4 to $6 million in sales. Rash firings and panic, while perhaps cathartic, aren't the answer. All you need to do is to add a layer of sales management and twenty-five new sales reps.

You can argue that small companies can't afford more than five reps. I argue they can't afford not to hire more reps.

It's possible to leverage your own reps with external sales structures. I consulted for a company, a recreational vehicle manufacturer that actually made it to $150 million with only five sales reps. This seemed impossible. Each rep selling $30 million worth of RVs? When I dug into it further, it turned out they had a lot more than five reps.

The company sold through retail RV dealers, each of which had a sales director and four sales reps. Five in-house reps oversaw 25 dealerships each with four reps, meaning 100 people were actually selling RVs. With $150 million in revenue, each person was selling about $1.5 million, a much more reasonable figure.

On the one hand, this was a very successful sales structure, leveraging five in-house reps into $150 million. On the other hand, they shouldn't have stopped at five, as their flat growth demonstrated.

CEOs seem to hate needing sales reps. They're expensive (actually they are free); they work too little (I doubt it); they drink too much (perhaps); and they project the wrong image of our company (what, profitable?). Maybe five reps are all some people can tolerate.

Instant Supply had 44 million sales reps. Well, okay, that was the number of catalogs that were mailed one year. They were Instant Supply's sales reps. Revenue exceeded $400 million ($2 billion in today's dollars).

CHAPTER 8

How Many Sales Reps
Do You Need?

Back in the late '80s, I was asked to speak at the Seattle meeting of the Direct Marketing Association, a small trade group of catalogers. I was genuinely looking forward to it, since it was the first time I had been invited to speak anywhere. It seemed Instant Supply, the catalog company I started, was suddenly an emerging star.

I happened to be vacationing in Astoria, Oregon (where *Goonies* was filmed). I rented a Cessna 172 to fly to Seattle (they were covering expenses, I thought). It was a beautiful day, and as I approached Puget Sound, I reveled in the scenery while panicking over what I was going to say.

I did a good job for my first speech: no fainting and minimal stuttering. During the Q&A, the first question came from a bespectacled man up front: "We mail a catalog four times per year. I noticed Instant Supply has monthly editions. What is the right mailing frequency, monthly or quarterly?" I stared at the man, the answer seemed incredibly obvious, "Catalog mailing frequency is too important a decision to leave up to the company, only the customer can decide that," I replied.

I now realized the man was asking a more basic question: "How many sales reps should I hire?" In our business, catalogs were our sales reps, and we reproduced those 44 million times each year. It's much the same today with web sales tools like Google Ad words. They're your digital reps. Your Google spend should be determined by your response rate not a decision by your head of marketing.

Whether he was asking: "What's the frequency I should mail my catalog?" or, "How many reps should I hire?" or, "How many Google ad words should I buy?" I couldn't answer the question. Only his customers could.

For some customers I mailed them the same catalog every week. Their purchasing behavior told me to. I don't know, and personally didn't care, if the strategy worked because I was always the top catalog in their in-box, or because they handed out all the extra copies, or because I inundated them into acquiescence. All I knew was that they were buying at an increased rate when I mailed more frequently. I let the customer vote with their dollars.

It is the same answer when you ask, "How many sales reps should I hire?" Hire sales reps until your customers no longer respond to more reps. At AsiaSoft, we've gone from five reps to 192 worldwide, and they still pay for themselves in six weeks. We are planning on doubling the sales force next year. At Social Advertising Corp., they pay for themselves in four weeks and they are adding a new sales office every other month. The customers are still affirming our hires by buying.

More is More

When I was an up-and-coming cataloger, I'd often quiz the CEOs of non-catalog companies. "What should a catalog company do to increase its sales?" Without exception, they would say, "Mail more catalogs." I don't remember a single CEO who said, "Invent new products," or "Lower your prices," or "Hire more engineers or product managers or purchasing agents." They just said, "Mail more catalogs," and they were right. More catalogs meant more sales. Of course, I also had to hire more customer service reps to take the orders and more warehouse workers to ship them, but the driving factor was the number of catalogs I mailed.

These CEOs understood my business intuitively, but somehow they couldn't apply the same logic to their own. Catalogs were my sales reps, and the CEOs suggested I send more without recognizing that by the same token, they should hire more sales reps if they wanted growth. Sales reps, real, printed, or virtual cause sales. And hiring real reps is actually a far better deal than mailing more catalogs:

- 97 to 98% of catalogs don't sell anything. Only 20% of sales reps fail.
- Catalogs stop selling in six weeks. Reps sell forever and at their maximum rate.
- Catalogs are static; everyone gets the same sales pitch. Reps can constantly adapt to their clients' needs.

• Sales reps can close $100,000 or $1,000,000 sales. A catalog probably can't sell much of anything over $1,000.

So why would CEOs so readily suggest sending more catalogs but not advocate rapid, aggressive sales rep hiring? I honestly don't know. But it's even stranger that when I asked catalog CEOs what direct selling companies should do to increase revenue, they would quickly answer, "Hire more sales reps." Maybe we should swap CEOs periodically. Or maybe it has something to do with forests and trees.

As it happens, the only time Instant Supply got into serious trouble was when we tried to be "efficient" in mailing catalogs. "Efficient" meant cutting the number of catalogs mailed, a decidedly bad idea. Regardless of the industry, sales reps cause sales and more is almost always better. CEOs need to internalize this idea.

An Acre of Cooks, But Only One Table

Imagine a restaurant with an enormous kitchen boasting three talented chefs, all the best equipment, and a bevy of sous-chefs. The kitchen is so grandiose, in fact, that it left room for only a handful of tables in the dining area. The food is marvelous of course, but the restaurant is destined to fail. There simply are not enough tables to support the cost of the kitchen. No matter how quickly they turn each table, even if they serve multiple parties at every meal, every day, they can't take in enough money to support the staff and rent. They don't have enough selling space.

Too many businesses are like this restaurant. They hire

engineers, financial staff, and HR, while neglecting their channel of distribution. You need to have enough sales resources to sustain everything else your company does. Sales is the engine that pulls the train; engineering, operations, finance, and administration are the boxcars. The greater the number of cars, the bigger the engine needs to be.

If you err in allocating resources, err in hiring too many sales reps. It works a lot better than too few.

How Many Sales Reps Should Sell an Engineer's Life Work, His Blood, His Sweat, and His Tears?

I love asking this question of VPs of Engineering and CEOs in Silicon Valley. I've never had anyone answer, "Fewer than one!" Yet most companies have more engineers than sales reps. Count the number of engineers in your company. Now count the number of feet on the street and divide by two. Does your company pass the test?

You should have multiple reps per engineer; that's how you leverage their work. That's where the profit is, and that's where the growth is. When you have the right sales rep to engineer ratio, your revenue per engineer goes through the roof.

Unfortunately, the mantra "Engineers are valuable; sales reps are expensive and don't work hard" persists in most CEOs' minds. I'm always amazed at their unflinching willingness to hire more engineers. I love engineers too. Some of my best friends are engineers. Come to think of it, I'm one. But compared to a

Figure 8.1 Return on Investment for a New Hardware Engineer

Quarter	Q1	Q2	Q3	Q4	Q5	Q6	Q7	Q8	Q9	Q10	Q11	Q12	Total
Revenue:													
New Product Revenue							$250,000	$250,000	$250,000	$250,000	$250,000	$250,000	$1,500,000
COGS (50%)							$125,000	$125,000	$125,000	$125,000	$125,000	$125,000	$750,000
Margin							$125,000	$125,000	$125,000	$125,000	$125,000	$125,000	$750,000
Expenses:													
Salary ($180,000/yr.)	$ 45,000	$45,000	$45,000	$45,000	$45,000	$45,000	$45,000	$45,000	$45,000	$45,000	$45,000	$45,000	$ 540,000
Benefits (25%)	$11,250	$11,250	$11,250	$11,250	$11,250	$11,250	$11,250	$11,250	$11,250	$11,250	$11,250	$11,250	$ 135,000
Overhead ($2,000/mo.)	$6,000	$6,000	$6,000	$6,000	$6,000	$6,000	$6,000	$6,000	$6,000	$6,000	$6,000	$6,000	$ 72,000
Total Cost	$62,250	$62,250	$62,250	$62,250	$62,250	$62,250	$62,250	$62,250	$62,250	$62,250	$62,250	$62,250	$ 747,000
Cash:													
Cash Flow Cumulative	($62,250)	($124,500)	($186,750)	($249,000)	($311,250)	($373,500)	($310,750)	($248,000)	($185,250)	($122,500)	($59,750)	$3,000	$3,000

60

sales rep, engineers are not as good an investment, still very good, but not as good.

Here's the math for engineers *(Figure 8.1, left)*: It generally takes about 18 months for a new engineer's project to get to market. This is changing with the internet and apps, but if you are developing hardware or enterprise software, it still is true. So assuming an $180,000 salary, plus 25% in benefits and $2,000 per month in office overhead, you've spent $373,000 before you have a chance to sell a dime. And even then, half of an engineer's products fail. If the product sells $1 million its first year and costs 50% to build, an engineer pays for himself in three years. Sales reps, on the other hand, pay for themselves in six weeks to six months or less and only cost $20,000 to $30,000 negative cash flow, one tenth of an engineer.

I was on the board of Graphic Soft, a graphic software company. Whenever I convinced them to hire even one additional sales rep, sales would go up, prompting the CEO to hire another five engineers, driving the company cash negative again. Graphic Soft could have been an incredible success if it had printed sales reps. Instead, it was only a good success. The VC was happy. The CEO retired. And all was well. They didn't know they could have been a billion dollar corporation. They had a great product, priced well in a rapidly expanding market. Hiring sales reps was proven to work in spades, but they just didn't do it.

How to Grow to $713,365,000 in Revenue in Two Years

If you want to grow exponentially, you need to hire sales reps exponentially. Double the sales force each year if you want to double sales each year. If you have a specific goal in mind, say $713,365,000 in revenue, you need to hire enough sales reps to get there. The number of sales rep you'll need is easy to calculate: divide $713,365,000 by your average sales per mature rep. Say that average is $275,000 per year; then the math is as follows:

Calculating the Number of Reps Needed

Figure 8.2 Number of Reps Needed to Reach $713,365,000 in revenue				
Revenue Target	/	Average Sales/Rep	=	# of Rep Needed
$ 713,365,000	/	$ 275,000	=	2,594

So you'll need 2,594 reps to get to $713,365,000 in revenue, assuming your mature reps average $275,000/year. I'll bet that's a lot fewer than you thought. Now let's say you're a very ambitious CEO and you decide to get to $713,365,000 in two years from startup, so you hire per the following schedule:

Figure 8.3 Hiring Schedule to Grow to $713,365,000 in Two Years								
Year	2009				2010			
Quarter	3/31	6/30	9/30	12/31	3/31	6/30	9/30	12/31
New Hires	2	16	28	48	80	1,201	371	2,202
Total Sales Reps	2	18	44	76	128	1,281	1,572	2,573

Essentially you hire 2,573 sales reps in eight quarters. Impossible, you say? The chart above (Figure 8.3) came from Groupon's S-1 for their 2012 IPO. The company's revenue after just two years in business was $713,365,000, an average of $277,250 per sales rep. I'll bet your reps are selling more than $277,250 per year. Maybe you want to hire 2,589 more sales reps to augment the five you have now. Stop reading this book, and start hiring.

		2009				2010			Total
Year		2009				2010			Total
Quarter	3/31	6/30	9/30	12/31	3/31	6/30	9/30	12/31	2010
Total Sales Reps	2	18	44	76	128	1,281	1,572	2,573	2,573
Sales Rep Growth %		800%	144%	73%	68%	901%	23%	64%	3286%
Revenue ($000)	$ 252	$ 3,301	$ 9,998	$ 16,920	$ 44,236	$ 87,298	$ 185,231	$ 396,600	$ 713,365
Revenue Growth %		1310%	303%	169%	261%	197%	212%	214%	2341%
Revenue/Rep ($000)	$ 126	$ 183	$ 227	$ 223	$ 346	$ 68	$ 118	$ 154	$ 277

Figure 8.4 Groupon Sales Hiring and Revenue Growth*

* Source: Groupon S1 Filing

It was a simple idea: email a coupon and they will come. What made this company special, and what made their CEO a billionaire in two years, is the fact he didn't decide how many sales reps to hire, his customers did. Groupon simply put the resources in place to let the market make them a success.

You can argue about Groupon's profitability, their product, and other aspects of their business, but as a revenue growth machine, they are to be admired.

Groupon recognized that sales reps cause sales, and hiring more became an intrinsic part of the company's culture. They erred on the side of hiring too many, creating a sales business supported by engineers, rather than an engineering business supported by five sales reps. Even as they grew, Groupon continued to hire reps exponentially. Eventually the market will stop responding to the new reps, and Groupon's hiring will reluctantly slow, but with a $7 billion corporate valuation so far, that day may still be far-removed.

Using the formula in Fig. 8.2, above, you can plan approximately how many reps you'll need to hit your revenue target. Beyond that, I can't tell you precisely how many reps you need for your specific company and circumstance; only your customers can. My advice is to follow Groupon's lead: hire sales reps until the model breaks, and then hire more to make sure the recent ones weren't just bad hires.

CHAPTER 9

When to Hire More

There are five common signs that you need to hire more sales reps.

1. Sales per rep are going up.

2. No sales reps are failing.

3. New product revenues are cannibalizing old product revenues.

4. Sales are clustered geographically around the rep's office.

5. VPs are blaming the economy for stalled growth.

1. Sales Per Rep Are Going Up

Most VPs and CEOs would be proud that their sales per rep are going up. Most boards would think it's a good thing. Yet it is the number one sign you are heading for a flat sales period.

A rising sales per rep average indicates that you are not adding enough sales horsepower for the coming year. Last year's hires are climbing the sales S-Curve, but you aren't hiring new ones who would drag the average down. Let me give you an example.

For simplicity, let's assume all reps are hired on January 1, and each performs per the Minicomputer Corp. S-Curve figures. Those are:

Figure 9.1 Minicomputer New Rep Sales Curve			
Year	1	2	3	4
Revenue	$ 200,000	$ 1,500,000	$ 3,000,000	$ 3,000,000

Now Let's Compare Two Companies.

Company A: Hires five reps first year and no further sales hiring.

Figure 9.2 Company A: Hire Five Reps First Year and No Further Hiring						
Year Hired	# of Reps Hired	Revenue	Year			
			1	2	3	4
1	5	From Reps Hired 1st Year	$ 1,000,000	$ 7,500,000	$ 15,000,000	$ 15,000,000
2	0	From Reps Hired 2nd Year				
3	0	From Reps Hired 3rd Year				
4	0	From Reps Hired 3rd Year				
		Total Company Revenue	$ 1,000,000	$ 7,500,000	$ 15,000,000	$ 15,000,000
		Revenue Growth Rate		650%	100%	0%
		Revenue/Sales Rep	$ 200,000	$ 1,500,000	$ 3,000,000	$ 3,000,000

Company B: Hires five reps first year, then doubling each year.

Figure 9.3 Company B - Hire Five Reps Initially then Doubling for Four Years						
Year Hired	# of Reps Hired	Revenue	Year			
			1	2	3	4
1	5	From Reps Hired 1st Year	$ 1,000,000	$ 7,500,000	$ 15,000,000	$ 15,000,000
2	10	From Reps Hired 2nd Year		$ 2,000,000	$ 15,000,000	$ 30,000,000
3	20	From Reps Hired 3rd Year			$ 4,000,000	$ 30,000,000
4	40	From Reps Hired 4th Year				$ 8,000,000
		Total Company Revenue	$ 1,000,000	$ 9,500,000	$ 34,000,000	$ 83,000,000
		Revenue Growth Rate		850%	258%	144%
		Revenue/Sales Rep	$ 200,000	$ 633,333	$ 971,429	$ 1,106,667

Note the bottom lines of Fig. 9.2 and 9.3. By year three, Company A's sales per rep are nearly triple those of Company B ($3,000,000 to $971,429). That's a good thing, right? Company A's sales department is three times as efficient, right? Yes they are, but the company is heading for a disaster and its rate of growth goes to zero in year four.

Look at year two: Company B's revenue is only slightly ahead of Company A's. But, by year four, B's revenue is more than 5X that of Company A's, and B has a growth rate of nearly 144% while A's has fallen to zero. This is because Company B is adding new reps that are still climbing the S-Curve and driving revenue growth. That's the critical difference.

Even if all hiring stops, what do you think happens in years five and six? Company A stays flat at $15 million in revenue. It is out of sales horsepower. Company B jumps to $175 million then $225 million+.

In year four would you have diagnosed Company A's sales hiring problem? If your sales went from $1 million to $7 million to $15 million and then flattened there, would you think to hire more sales reps? Most CEOs don't think it's a sales hiring issue. They think it is a lazy sales rep issue, or a bad engineering department issue, or disastrous marketing department issue.

You need to consider how many reps you'll need for your targeted future revenue. If you want to grow into a $1 billion company like Groupon, then you need the number of sales reps equal to $1 billion divided by your average mature sales rep's revenue. (This average won't change much, so you don't want to forecast based on it going up.)

EduSoft had eight reps covering the US and could not conceive of having 40 reps ever, yet they wanted to grow to $1 billion in revenue. That would mean $125,000,000 per sales rep. There are countries with smaller GDPs than that. Make sure your sales hiring matches your revenue aspirations, especially if you are spending to those aspirations in non-sales departments.

2. No Sales Reps Are Failing

I remember someone asking the VP of Sales at Minicomputer Corp., "How did you build such a great sales force?" He said, "Hire lots, lose lots." He actually said, "Hire lots, fire lots," but that was too politically incorrect to put in this book, so I won't.

Minicomputer Corp. did have a lot of failing sales reps. It's inevitable when you hire so aggressively. And Minicomputer Corp. planned it that way. Their commission plan had a very low base, so under-performing reps didn't cost them much. Since those reps couldn't eat very well on a low base, they typically moved to sales jobs at HP which had a higher base and a capped commission. Minicomputer Corp. had the lowest base with no cap on commission. Thus, while the lower performing sales reps fled, the best and brightest stayed and became the highest-compensated sales force in the industry. (Alas, the sales force was later destroyed by a change in the comp plan, more on that later.)

Sales should involve some natural selection. If every rep is succeeding, then you're not hiring fast enough. That is the perfect time to hire more reps. Hire more until selling your product is no longer like shooting fish in a barrel. Your revenue will go up. Some reps will fail. And because they fail, you will know you have at least enough sales reps for the market environment.

If you don't have any failing sales reps, you are grossly understaffed.

3. New Product Revenues Are Cannibalizing Old Product Revenues

EduSoft, the educational hardware company, encountered this problem. Founded by two engineers, EduSoft made small, battery-operated educational computers for classrooms. Designed and priced to make computers more available to kids, EduSoft's devices came in carts of 20 which could be rolled from class to class. It was an excellent concept, and the initial model sold well.

When EduSoft sales flattened, they introduced a follow-on model with several incremental improvements and a higher price. Personally, I didn't think the improvements justified the higher price, but it was newer technology, and their customers were spending taxpayer's money (read: they weren't very price sensitive). The new model sold well, but the company saw no revenue growth. As sales of the new model rose, they almost exactly offset the declining sales of the old model. Total revenue remained flat.

This scared the two founders and major shareholder; 99% of the founder's net worth was on the line. Prior to this product launch they thought all their selling problems could be solved in the lab, where they were more comfortable. Now they were perplexed. Why had their improvements continued stagnation instead of sparking growth?

Figure 9.4 New Product Sales Cannibalizing
Old Product Sales Due to Lack of Sales Bandwidth

The introduction of the new product had exposed their lack of selling horsepower.

When a company introduces a significant new product while its predecessor products are still selling well, one would expect growth to result. When growth doesn't result, there is usually a brief period of uncertainty, followed by sentiments like: "It was lucky we introduced the new product when we did, or our sales would be down 50%." No, if the new product wasn't introduced, your sales would have stayed the same. You had a limited supply of sales calls, and you just switched them from selling the old product to selling the new product, which is easier to sell because it's "better, faster, and smarter".

If you have strong existing products and are launching a new product, you need enough sales resources to push both simultaneously, rather than letting the new simply cannibalize the old resulting in no growth.

4. Sales Are Clustered Geographically Around the Reps

If you don't already, you should plot your sales by sales office location. Understanding your sales geography is important to getting comfortable hiring more reps. It's also useful when planning new sales offices.

EduSoft had eight sales reps nationwide doing $29 million in total revenue. One rep was doing in excess of $8 million herself. Her territory was Texas to Minnesota, west to Denver and east

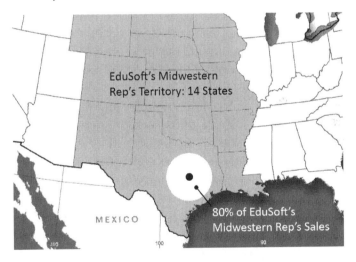

Fig. 9.5 80% of Midwest's Rep's sales were within 150 miles of her office.

to Dubuque, a significant chunk of the country. Yet when I plotted her sales by customer location, which the company had never done, I found that over 80% of her sales ($6.5 million) were within 150 miles of her home office in Texas. She had a territory nearly the size of the Louisiana Purchase but did almost all her selling in a local area about the size of Rhode Island. Imagine if the company had enough reps to service her entire territory that well.

If one rep can sell $6.5 million in a local area, why give her 1/3rd of the continental US? I advised EduSoft to divide up its territories and hire more reps to service them. The market could clearly support it. Management was surprisingly reluctant to do this, but sales soared when they finally did. Having never graphed their sales geographically, they hadn't known this opportunity was there. They believed their territories were performing well. In reality, they were dramatically under-served and ripe for new reps and more revenue.

I had an under-served territory myself when I was a sales rep at Minicomputer Corp. My territory stretched from Palo Alto to the Washington border, yet the year I sold $10 million ($50,000,000 in 2013 dollars), I did not have a sale more than one mile from my office. I had three customers on our block. If not for Stanford University being one mile away, all my sales would have been within ¼ mile of our office. Minicomputer Corp. understood this. They graphed their sales by geography. The following year the company added Portland and Seattle sales offices.

If your profitable territories are not being completely covered, the most important thing you can do is hire more reps.

5. Management Is Blaming the Economy

Selling problems are often misdiagnosed. CEOs and VPs, I find, usually blame either engineering or marketing: engineering because they are almost always behind schedule and marketing because you can't really tell if they're doing any good. (Sales tends to avoid blame because they are at least bringing in orders.) But very often executives place blame outside the company altogether, citing the market, the economy, or anything else not under their or the company's control. "If we can't do anything about it, it's not our fault." This is the most dangerous reason because it breeds acceptance of your fate and not control over it.

The bad news is it probably is your fault. The good news is that means you can do something about it. Hire more reps. Here's a good example, also from EduSoft.

At EduSoft the mantra was that educational budgets were being severely cut. "How can the Board expect us to grow in this environment," they protested. I argued that EduSoft was such a small part of the market, and thus, educational budgets did not matter much. When my argument didn't sell, I dug into the educational market data further. I found that educational budgets were actually growing at 8% per year and had been for the past ten years in a row. The "cuts" were "government cuts" which doesn't mean actual spending cuts; they mean cuts from projected increases. In fact, it was the largest sustained growth in federal education spending ever, especially for technology. EduSoft, by blaming the environment, were simply claiming to be victims, when all they needed was more sales reps.

Management has strong motivations to blame "the market" for a sales problem. When you hear such a scapegoat, it's time for introspection…and then more sales hiring.

CHAPTER 10

How to Get New Customers

My advice is simple for getting new customers: hire new sales reps in new territories.

If you have a competitive product or service, priced well, in a large and growing market, then hiring new sales reps in new territories will get you new customers. **Sales reps cause sales, new sales reps cause new customer sales.**

When I joined Minicomputer Corp., they had sold zero computers in my territory (Palo Alto, CA to the Washington border) in the two previous years. That year I closed 19 new accounts, three times more than any other Minicomputer Corp. sales rep. In a way, I had to. I had just purchased a house, had a pregnant wife, and needed much more money than Minicomputer Corp.'s base salary of $16,000 per year ($85,000 in 2012 dollars).

Mortgage and baby motivation aside, I had a lot of advantages. I was a decent sales rep. I had tons of time, since there were no existing customers bugging me. I had knowledge from my experience in computer marketing at two other companies. And, I had an untapped territory that included Stanford University, Aero Corp., US Geological Service, and Stanford Research Institute all within five miles of my office. If I was willing to drive (I wasn't), I also had Bank of America, Chevron, Levi Strauss, Clorox and more, all just in the Bay Area alone.

Yet only two years after my 19 new customer performance, I would land zero new customers. It's not that I floundered; it was that I was out of time. Aero Corp. had placed the largest order in the history of my company. SRI bought a large system. Five Stanford departments had bought systems, and I had uncovered two major OEM accounts, accounts that designed our computer into their systems and resold them. I was buried just getting my company to ship, fix and support my customers. The last thing I had time for was new customer prospecting.

Why New Reps in New Areas Cause New Business

They can't help it. They need commission and they have time to make new customer calls.

When AsiaSoft hired three reps in London, largely to shut me up, one rep booked a $400,000 new customer order within three weeks.

Previously confined to Miami, Social Advertising Corp. opened a Chicago sales office. During their first month, the rookie sales team booked more business than the experienced reps in Miami, and it was all from new customers.

Likewise, when I moved to the north of England to set up Instant Supply, my first mailing yielded $16.00 per catalog mailed in revenue. Comparable US mailings returned only $0.75 per catalog mailed. I had to stop mailing because I blew through six months of inventory in six weeks. And they were all new customers.

You may recall EduSoft's $8 million rep. Her territory was 14 states. She had only one sale outside of Texas, and 12 states where she sold nothing. The company promoted her and added five sales reps under her, each assigned a portion of the 12 untouched states. Her territory went from $8 million to $15 million in one year. And the $7 million growth was all new customers from untapped states.

To get new customers, you have to hire new reps. To get a lot of new customers, you have to hire a lot of new reps in new territories.

Why Current Reps Can't and Shouldn't Sell New Customers

Many CEOs are extremely frustrated by their experienced sales reps. Instead of appreciating their steady stream of business, CEOs are bugged that their sales reps are not bringing in new customers. "They just aren't working hard enough. We need to push them harder; they are too comfortable." While perhaps cathartic, this mindset is very wrong.

If you stop and think about what you really want your reps to do, it should be:

1. Don't lose an existing customer.

2. Sell more to an existing customer.

3. Get new customers.

Existing customers are and should be the primary focus of experienced reps. A sale is not a one-time event. After a customer orders the first time, they expect good service, on-time deliveries, support, and such. In short, they need your rep's time. A big customer is even worse. They expect miracles and they want your sales rep to perform them. The grass always looks greener with another supplier.

In my third year at Minicomputer Corp., I was down to three customers and I was buried. I felt like a hamster on a wheel. I'd have one group waiting in a conference room, while I was meeting with another group next door. I was so busy, the company eventually gave me my own assistant at the factory. I had three customers and no time to get new ones. Luckily, my company only wanted me to keep the customers I had happy and buying. They understood.

Mature reps simply run out of time. And just as this causes their revenue to plateau atop the S-Curve, it also makes their new customer acquisition trend toward zero. Trust me, that is not only okay, it should be what you want.

The Inverted New Customer S-Curve

A sales rep's rate of new customer acquisition goes down each year. That's why you need to keep hiring new reps if you want to continue to get new customers. Consider my new customer acquisition curve at Minicomputer Corp.

Figure 10.1 Number of new customers from date of hire
at MiniComputer Corp.

I closed no new customers in my third year. Instead, I made sure my three customers had their problems solved, and kept ordering in large quantities. Thus, my revenue curve was a mirror image of my customer acquisition curve:

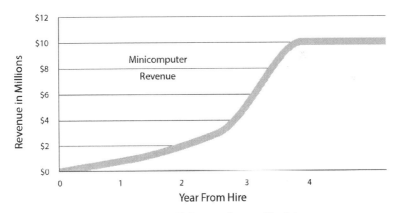

Figure 10.2 My Revenue from my Hire Date
at Minicomputer Corp.

If I had stayed a fourth year, my revenue would have been flat at $10 million just like my customer acquisition was flat at zero. I was out of time. Minicomputer Corp. paid me $252,000 that third year ($1,500,000 in 2012 dollars), a cost of selling of 2.52%. A Minicomputer Corp. rep booking $1 million, which was considered very good performance, cost the company $52,500 or 5.25%, twice what I cost per dollar. In other words, I was both the highest-grossing, cheapest, and most profitable sales rep, but I closed no new customers and had no revenue growth.

Mature reps are the best deal, but as their revenue goes up, their new customer acquisition goes down. You have to augment them with new reps to continue to grow. And with a great sales comp plan your mature sales reps are making a lot of money and are locked into your company and your customers.

Why New Customers Are Even More Important Than CEOs Think

Every CEO wants tons of new customers. But I don't know if they fully appreciate how valuable those new customers are over the span of their relationship with their company.

In most industries, new customers follow a purchasing S-Curve. If you graph your sales data, you can reasonably predict how much a new customer will buy in years two and three, just as you can predict what your average rep will sell in years two and three. You can also predict the customer's total lifetime purchases. These figures are very valuable for a CEO to know well. It will help you decide how much to invest in new customers acquisition.

Given the S-Curve, new customers start slow, but in the long run they are a cash cow. They're worth sacrificing for. They're worth hiring for. Just look at the purchasing S-Curve for a new customer at AsiaSoft:

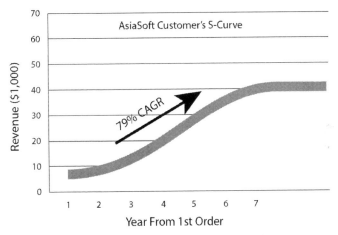

Figure 10.3 AsiaSoft New Customer Growth S-Curve

An $8,000 new customer in year one yields over $100,000 of revenue total by year five. Don't you think you should start hiring new sales reps now to get more new customers climbing the S-Curve now?

CHAPTER 11

How Many Sales Offices Do You Need

*"At the risk of jeopardizing my job, what am
I supposed to be doing?"
-- Office Soft Corp.'s future best sales rep*

Not long ago, I had dinner with a major bank CEO. At dinner he started telling stories about the early days of his firm.

> When George and I started iBank in San Jose, we grew pretty quickly. As a result, the SEC required us to have more "good" capital on hand. Somewhat out of desperation, George called his uncle in Austin to ask for a loan. His uncle said, "Sure, but you have to put a branch in Austin first."
>
> That turned out be a major key to our success. Our sales in the Austin area more than doubled. It didn't make sense. All discount brokers operated by telephone. All our other competitors were

centralized. Why would a local branch matter? We weren't sure, but we were smart enough to notice the huge increase in sales in Austin, and we started branching rapidly.

Recently, I pushed one of my consulting clients to imitate iBank's model. They had one centralized sales office in Miami. At my urging, they opened a sales office in Chicago. Their sales in Illinois promptly doubled. In chatting with their Illinois sales reps, I asked if they ever mentioned their location. The reps responded, "Only if the customer is located in Illinois."

Local presence matters. I always push for geographically-dispersed sales offices. Err on the side of having more, smaller offices in disparate places, because people like to do business with someone local, even if it's just one guy with a phone and a chair.

Why a One-Man Sales Office Works

At Office Soft Corp., a retail small business software firm, we added a one-man sales office in Boca Raton, Florida to call on only one customer: Office Depot. It was the best move we ever made. Though admittedly, it seemed a bit crazy at the time. We could only meet with Office Depot's buyer quarterly, and we had an annual contract renegotiation at Consumer Electronics Show in Las Vegas. But we parked someone there full-time anyway.

After a month on the job, George, the rep nobly manning our lonely outpost, called and asked: "At the risk of jeopardizing my job, what am I supposed to be doing? I can only meet with the buyer once every three months."

I answered: "Get to know the other buyers; they rotate every two years. Take the PR department to lunch. Chat with operations to make sure we're doing everything right. Get to know the receptionist to find out when our competitors are visiting. Talk to promotions, advertising, and IT departments. Play golf with anyone with an Office Depot business card."

George loved golf and did this with gusto, (after all, he didn't have much else to do) and the results were amazing. Soon Office Depot's promotions department started calling George saying: "Can you fill an end cap in two weeks? We just had a vendor cancel next month's end cap promotion. Normally it costs $80,000, but it's free if you can do it."

Their PR department called and said: "Business Week is doing a story, and they want to interview a vendor. Can you run over? They're here now."

When the new software buyer was appointed, George had just played golf with him the prior week. We were way ahead of the curve at this account.

Setting up George as a one man shop was a small investment that paid off big for us, and his golf handicap went down. True, Office Depot was a large potential account so we could afford to dedicate someone to it. But it's just as easy to dedicate someone to a new territory.

One-man sales offices can excel in markets that you may not otherwise even access. And they're very efficient. One person in an office has nobody to chat with except the customer.

Why a Six Person Office Is Second Best

A sales manager can only effectively manage five reps, something I discussed in Chapter 7, "The Rule of Five". Unless you add another layer of sales management, the sixth rep will likely fail. Thus, the six-person sales office–five reps plus one manager–is the best alternative to the one-man office. IBM had a five man sales office when I was an intern there. That was many years ago.

Office sizes should grow as a multiple of the Rule of Five. So after six-person sales offices, the next optimal size jumps to thirty-one: one branch manager, five group managers and twenty-five sales reps reporting to them. At the risk of insulting your intelligence, here's the organization chart for a thirty-one-person office.

		Regional Office Mgr		
District Sales Mgr 1	District Sales Mgr 2	District Sales Mgr 3	District Sales Mgr 4	District Sales Mgr 5
Sales Rep 1	Sales Rep 1	Sales Rep 1	Sales Rep 1	Sales Rep 1
Sales Rep 2	Sales Rep 2	Sales Rep 2	Sales Rep 2	Sales Rep 2
Sales Rep 3	Sales Rep 3	Sales Rep 3	Sales Rep 3	Sales Rep 3
Sales Rep 4	Sales Rep 4	Sales Rep 4	Sales Rep 4	Sales Rep 4
Sales Rep 5	Sales Rep 5	Sales Rep 5	Sales Rep 5	Sales Rep 5
Figure 11.1 Thirty-One Person Sales Office Organization Chart				

The real question is: "Are you better off with twenty-five sales reps in one office or five offices with five reps each?" It's no contest. Five offices gets you five more local geographies that will double or triple in sales, and the cost of personnel and overhead is about the same. In fact, five offices may be cheaper. Somehow a thirty-one-person office needs assistants, facilities managers, maybe even HR. The five person offices are lean and have lower travel expenses since your reps are closer to your customers.

Moreover, dispersing your operations will improve decision making. The manager of a six person office can't bump a decision up to anybody; nobody's there to bump it to. He has to make decisions and he gets to see the results of those decisions. Running a small office is great management training that you don't get in a centralized organization. This alone would make me want to be decentralized.

How Zip Codes Help You Sell More

In Chapter 10, I suggested plotting your sales by location so you can tell when you need more reps by exposing uncovered territories. Well, it can also inform your decision about where to open new sales offices.

EduSoft didn't have a rep located in California or New York, the two biggest education markets. I argued that they needed a minimum of fifty reps just to service the Departments of Education in each state. This was a perfect opportunity for small, distributed offices.

As an aside, we did learn one other interesting fact from plotting EduSoft's sales. It turned out the Georgia rep sold far more in North Carolina than Georgia. At first I couldn't figure out why. Was the market better in North Carolina? Was it the demographics? The weather? Then I asked the rep herself. Reluctantly, and only with my promise not to tell the company, she said: "Oh, I've been living with my fiancée in North Carolina. I spend a lot more time there than Georgia." So graphing your sales geography not only tells you where to put your new sales offices, it can tell you where to send your wedding gifts too.

We didn't have a choice at Instant Supply. We were going to run out of mailing lists we could rent in the US. We knew that mailing to proven lists worked; we just needed more proven lists. So we duplicated the company in Europe and Japan. It worked beautifully.

Thirty years later, I still have a hard time convincing American CEOs to open international sales offices. When I suggest Europe or Asia, they try to pacify me by suggesting Australia or Canada, which I suppose seem more familiar or American-like. Australia has a population of 22 million, about two-thirds that of California. Their GDP is $924 billion, less than one-seventeenth the size of the European Union (World Bank, 2009). Familiarity is great, but it's not necessarily the most profitable course.

At AsiaSoft, after four Board meetings listening to me harp about Europe being a bigger market for their software than America, the CEO announced he had just hired a firm to sell for them in the UK. It was clearly done to shut me up, a reasonable motivation, I admit. Three weeks later, one of the UK reps closed a $400,000 order, paying for the company's international expansion for the entire year. Now 30% of AsiaSoft's revenue comes from Europe, with offices in Paris, Munich, and London and another 25% comes from Asia, which given their name, seems logical. They did open the requisite office in Australia and Canada first. Those offices produce less than 2% of their revenue.

Groupon's Secret

Groupon's 3,665 sales reps are located in 74 offices. They put in 74 offices in 2.75 years. The first remote branch is the hardest. After that it's a recipe.

At Instant Supply, once we successfully put a branch in New Jersey to complement our Silicon Valley operation, we knew we could go global. Putting a branch in London, Paris, or Tokyo was not much different. AsiaSoft found that creating a branch in Singapore or Munich was much the same as doing it in Chicago. Being able to manage remote operations successfully became a major weapon, just as it was to iBank, or Groupon, Instant Supply Catalog, or Ray Kroc, founder of McDonald's.

Initially, my partner at Instant Supply didn't see the need for a branch in New Jersey, let alone Europe. "Okay, we can set up these offices, but how will I know they're not stealing from me?" I think this was his excuse to avoid branching. I've heard many, but he had a valid point, so I said: "How do you know they aren't stealing from you here? Can you look through walls? Can you see that case of floppy disks walking out the back door right now?"

The irony is that three years and eight branches later, the only theft we ever found was at our original location in Sunnyvale. And the controls to uncover it probably never would have been put in place if we hadn't branched.

Don't Be a Perennial Bachelor

"Yes, I'll marry you, just not now."

Remote sales offices will never be easier to establish than now.

When it comes to decentralizing your sales offices, the bigger you are, the harder it is. If iBank hadn't been forced to branch early, if my partner hadn't agreed to branch early, he would still be saying, "Yes, Bill, I agree decentralization is better, just not now."

I saw the results of the "not right now" mentality years ago at a large centralized clothing cataloger. Since I was a cataloger and sat on the board of another catalog company, we had a meeting at their corporate headquarters and got a tour of their operation.

During their rapid growth phase, they attached new buildings to the back of their existing facility. This continued year after year, creating what I can only call a monstrosity. I could just hear the management discussions: "Yes, we should put a new sales office and distribution facility in Florida, California, Texas or wherever, just not now."

You had to walk through three or four buildings to get to the boots and then another three buildings to get to the sweaters. Even if they had a product in stock when a customer ordered, they couldn't ship it for two weeks. Compare that to a one-man operation that could do it in five minutes, or a 31 person Instant Supply branch that could do it the same day, or distributed Amazon warehouses that do it same day. Incredibly, this cataloguer's computer system actually delayed orders from being printed for one week, so all the boots "Style 1234" or the sweaters "Style 4567" could be pulled at once.

Just consider the distances. At Instant Supply you had to walk 100 feet maximum to reach either end of any of our 29 warehouses. At the centralized facility, honestly, I think you could've gotten lost before you found the end. Big and centralized is horribly inefficient, especially for fulfillment and certainly for sales offices. Commit to decentralizing.

Keep it small and replicate. You already know how to manage that size facility. Why change? Ray Kroc did it with McDonald's. Once he successfully put in his first remote McDonald's, all he had to do was to do it again and again and again 30,000+ times. That's a lot easier than the need to invent something new or manage something bigger.

CHAPTER 12

The Value of On-Time Hiring

"Sales Reps don't sell much if you haven't hired them yet."
-- VP of Sales at Minicomputer Corp.

The first question Minicomputer Corp's VP of Sales asked his Branch Sales Managers was, "Are you on your sales rep hiring plan?" He asked about revenue next. He is the only VP of Sales I had ever heard do that. He understood better than anyone that delayed sales hiring would delay sales, which would reduce growth, and cause his stock options to go down. He didn't like that.

At Instant Supply, if I didn't mail a catalog, I wouldn't get any orders. If my business sells through Google ads, I won't sell anything until I actually place those ads. It's the same concept when you sell through sales reps: you won't get any new business until you actually hire them. Every day you wait costs you money.

Delayed Hiring Disaster

Every product, no matter how ground-breaking or fashionable, will eventually become obsolete. The selling time frame is finite. And not only is the end inevitable, it's determined by factors beyond your control: market changes, competition, new technology, the wane of a once-promising fad, etc. The end date is set and you can't change it.

Let's say the average s competitive life of your products is 36 months (length of time that a new customer would choose that product), and the profit curve for your product looks something like this:

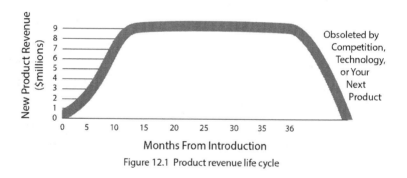

Figure 12.1 Product revenue life cycle

What happens if you delay the product's introduction by 6 months? You get the profit curve in Figure 12.2, below.

Your window of opportunity is going to close at month 36 regardless of what you do. So a six month delay costs you six months of mature product sales. In this case that's about a 16% loss in revenue, even more in product profit. The market gives you a finite time period and you have to exploit it.

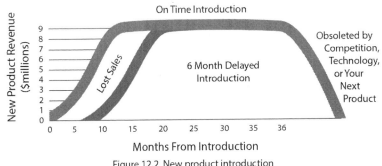

Figure 12.2 New product introduction

Oddly enough, the same is true for sales reps. Every rep you hire may eventually leave, for reasons largely beyond your control: to move to another state, to raise a child, for a better job offer etc. You have a finite amount of time to benefit from their sales. And a hiring delay, just like a product launch delay, costs you mature sales. This is because every rep starts slowly, working up the S-Curve. That slow start, be it six weeks or six months, is unavoidable and the rep's departure date is effectively set, so the only variable is the amount of time atop the S-Curve. The sooner you hire the longer that will be.

You're losing money every day you're not hiring; it just happens to be next year's or next quarter's money.

On-the-Shelf Hiring

My boss at Minicomputer Corp. had two or three sales reps ready to come on board at any moment. They were on-the-shelf, queued to join. And the day a hiring authorization was issued, he had a new rep selling in minutes not months.

93

Compare that to most sales managers. If managers have an authorized hire date of March 1st, they don't really start thinking about looking until March 1st. They don't have serious candidates until May 1st and don't hire until September 30th, thereby losing seven months of mature sales revenue. Yes, March 1 to September 30 is seven months of lost revenue.

The reason my boss hired so diligently is not just that he was a great sales manager, though he was; it's that he was highly incentivised to do it. He got paid a percentage of all the sales booked by his reps, as most sales managers do, and the percentage was graduated based on the average sales per rep. So if his reps averaged $100,000, he got a .50% commission. If his reps averaged $500,000, he got 1.5%±:

Figure 12.3 Minicomputer's Sales Manager Commission	
Sales/Rep	Commission Rate
0 to $100,000	0.50%
100,001 to $200,000	0.75%
$200,001 to $400,000	1.00%
$400,000+	1.50%

The secret was that an authorization to hire a rep was counted the same as a rep. So if he had three sales reps in the territory and one authorization to hire, his revenue was divided by four, not three, to determine the average sales per rep. An empty seat devastated his average. My boss therefore had to hire on time if he wanted to make more money. It was a brilliantly effective tactic for Minicomputer Corp.

At AsiaSoft, the company sales managers get $50 per month deducted from their commission check for each non-hired sales rep. It's not the fine that motivates, but the monthly report telling the CEO who's being charged the fine. The message is clear: management is watching your hiring plan. Before this simple addition to the comp plan, AsiaSoft was 40 reps behind in hiring on a base of 90, which greatly reduced their growth. The CEO caught it and fixed it. Love that CEO.

One of my consulting clients recently implemented a strong disincentive to hire. I hate it, but I couldn't stop it. If a manager has no reps under him, he is paid a $1,000 bonus per new customer. If he has one rep, he is paid $750, and with two reps, $500. Knowing sales managers as well as I do, I know exactly what will happen: they won't hire. There will perpetually be one or two accounts about to close, and the manager will rationalize not hiring until after they do. I'll report in the second edition (assuming I hire enough reps to sell this book that I have a second edition) on the results. They won't be good.

Hiring Google

"Hi Bill, this is Alex Doll. I worked with you at Palo Alto Electronics in the '80s. I've started a company and we have no revenue. Can you come down and talk to us? You seemed to understand something about marketing and sales." Alex Doll? I hadn't talked to the guy in thirty years, but apparently that hadn't dissuaded him. I was intrigued and bored. So, I went to see Alex and his partner Larry.

They had invented a new pressure transducer, which is engineering jargon for a device that measures pressure or weight. If you placed a brick on it, the capacitance changed and they could convert this change to weight. It was cheap and reasonably effective. Later McDonald's bought lots of them to measure the amount of CO_2 in their soda tanks eliminating many CO_2 deliveries that were not needed.

After five minutes with Alex and Larry, I determined why they hadn't sold any—they had no one selling. Egregious yes, but at least it was a problem I could help them solve.

The key was to get these transducers designed into products and hopefully those products would sell well, similar to selling an integrated circuit to Apple to be built into every iPhone. I figured if I were an engineer looking for a pressure transducer, I would probably start by Googling "pressure transducer". So I asked Bill and Larry if they had tried Google Adwords. They didn't know what Google Adwords was, which to be fair, was understandable since this was a few years ago.

I sat down in front of them and, in five minutes, wrote and launched an ad on Google. It went live about three minutes later. That is eight minutes to hire a sales rep. With one more click I could hire thousands more. We spent the rest of the hour looking at their product and reminiscing about the good-old days at Palo Alto Electronics. As I was leaving, I suggested we look at the Google ad results. There were, if I recall, four requests for samples from around the world. We paid 10 cents per click, or a total of 40 cents for four potential new customers in one hour. Those early Google prices seem so quaint now.

In the next month, Alex and Larry's Google AdWords landed them 3,000 inquiries and four or five design wins per month.

Regretfully, their product didn't meet spec and they had to resort to selling gross measurement transducers with $+/-$ two pound accuracy. Still, they had a good market, like the McDonald's CO_2 tanks.

Alex and Larry were lucky. Their product could be sold directly over the web with AdWords that took effect almost immediately. This allowed them to weather a very late and tentative sales start. But if you can't sell directly over the web, if your product requires physical sales reps, then you have to start hiring early because reps take time to mature. CEOs tend to think they can delay hiring reps since they don't generate anything for the first four months anyway. No, it's the opposite. You can delay AdWords and other direct sales efforts, as Alex and Larry proved, but with reps you have to be early and vigilant. It takes much longer to cover the lost ground if you're not.

Terminating Too Early

When I was in marketing at Rugged Computer Corp., they terminated our new LA sales rep, Mike. I thought he was a star, but he hadn't booked anything in the five months he'd been with the company, and he was driving us all nuts with questions and requests from his potential customers. So he got canned. The following month, seven major orders came in from his erstwhile territory. Turns out, the sales cycle for our rugged computers was six months long. Mike's seeds were finally sprouting. At our next staff meeting the VP of Sales declared, without a hint of irony: "If I hadn't terminated Mike, we never would have gotten these orders. He just couldn't sell and I had to close these all myself."

I rolled my eyes. Mike went onto a great sales career at our competitor.

Reps take time to mature. The S-Curve delay is precisely why you've got to be very impatient in hiring reps but patient in managing them once you do. You want to maximize the time they're selling at peak with your company, not cut them off before they get to peak.. Don't wait to hire, but do wait to fire.

SECTION 3

HOW TO
MOTIVATE

CHAPTER 13

How to Write a Great Sales Compensation Plan

Your sales compensation plan is one of the most important determinants of your company's success. And as such, one of the most important jobs of the CEO is to develop and protect the sales comp plan.

I've always said, "Show me your sales comp plan and I will tell you exactly what your reps are doing." How you set up your comp plan tells you sales reps how they should behave and whether to drive growth or not.

Yes, the comp plan is the CEO's responsibility, in collaboration with the VP of Sales and specifically not with the VP of HR or Finance. It is a key business strategy, as key as your product plan, your engineering plan, or your marketing plan. Most companies and CEOs don't assign this level of importance to it, but they should. The comp plan is one of the two keys to hyper sales growth. The other is hiring enough reps.

When you develop your comp plan, you should do it with the

intent of not changing it for the next five to ten years. It's not that you can't change it, but if you tell yourself you can't change the plan for ten years, you will assign its development the importance it deserves and requires. Developing your plan is a very difficult task and an important opportunity.

Before you start developing a comp plan, it's key to consider the motivations of the people involved. What does a sales rep want from his comp plan and what do you, as CEO, want?

- CEOs want predictable, growing, profitable sales revenue with controllable selling costs.

- Sales reps want control of their own destiny and to be compensated for their efforts without debate.

Thankfully, these are not mutually exclusive.

10 Rules Your Compensation Plan Must Meet

These rules are very important to incorporate in your plan:

1. Provides predictable, reliable commissions.
2. Motivates reps to invest in their territory across years.
3. Has uncapped commissions.
4. Retains your great reps.
5. Pays more per dollar sold to those who sell more.
6. Treats each dollar of revenue as a dollar of revenue.

7. Ensures current customers are treated better than new ones.

8. Controls the cost of selling.

9. Aligns rep and management motivations.

10. Gives your reps and managers incremental reasons to hustle.

1. Provides Predictable, Reliable Commission Payments

Your commission plan should be clear, simple, and easy to calculate. You, as CEO, should be able to do it. Accounting should be able to do it. The rep should be able to do it. And everyone should come up with the same answer. The best way to assure the commission calculation is straightforward is to attach three examples to the plan itself. You, the CEO, should do these example calculations.

Do not renegotiate or rationalize paying less commission after the sale. Nothing destroys sales motivation more, not only for the rep in question, but for all of his or her colleagues. At one of my companies the CEO said, "We can pay him $100,000, not the $300,000 the plan calls for." I calmly stated, okay maybe not so calmly stated, "Not only should you pay him, you should pay him in front of the entire company and throw in a car to boot." They did, and were amazed that the other sales reps were now coming in two hours early and staying late.

2. Motivates Reps to Invest in Their Territory Across Years

This seems an obvious goal for a sales comp plan, but most plans don't achieve it, especially those that pay as a percent of quota that is reset annually. It may take from 6 months to three years for a rep to climb the S-Curve. When they get there, they want to be paid. If you pay as a percentage of quota, you will increase your rep's quota each year and drive your best reps out of your company.

Design your plan to pay the same now for a dollar of revenue as you will three years from now. And never have a plan that uses judgment instead of math. By judgment I mean, "He sold $2,000,000 last year, so let's give him a quota of $3,000,000 this year."

3. Has Uncapped Commissions

Sales reps accept the risk that they won't make much money if they don't sell, so they want to believe the sky is the limit if they do sell. Capping commission takes that highly motivational dream away.

Most CEOs believe in uncapped commissions. They believe they already have an uncapped plan. They don't. Most plans are only uncapped during a single commission year. The plans get reset every January 1st by increasing the successful reps' revenue targets. This is wrong. You should pay for revenue and not for achieving a percentage of a target. This concept will become clearer in the next chapter.

Usually a recurring sale that rep made last year will pay him significantly less this year, because, as one VP of Sales said about her best rep, "You can bet her quota will be going up next year."

To test your plan, imagine you are a rep and you sell a new

customer $30,000 this year, $1,000,000 next year and $3,000,000 the following year. What would your company's plan pay you? If your plan doesn't pay you at least 100X or more in the third year for this 100X revenue increase, then your plan is capped. Fix it.

4. Retains Your Great Reps

Most comp plans drive great reps out of the company, primarily because of percent-of-quota based comp plans illustrated in the next chapter.

Your plan should pay more per dollar sold to your great reps, not differentiate between new and current customers, and enable your reps to harvest and get paid for all the work they have done in the prior years.

A friend, selling computers for a startup, focused on companies that would design his computers into their products and, hopefully, sell tons for him sometime in the future. He did this because he trusted his company to pay him three years from now for the seed work he was doing now. They did and became a billion dollar plus company. My friend bought a Ferrari and stayed with the company for over ten years.

Just the other day when I was helping a another startup's new VP Sales design a commission plan; he suggested, "Why don't we do a plan that pays as a percentage of quota each year, like the one I was on at my old job?"

I replied, "Those plans drive your best reps out of the company."

As the light went on, he sighed, "You mean, like it just did to me?" He had been a top sales manager at a major microcomputer company, until the comp plan forced him to leave. Of course, the mediocre sales reps still work there because their quotas are not going up.

Early in my career, I set up a comp plan for my outbound catalog sales people. They called major companies, negotiated discounts, collected engineers' names to receive catalogs, and helped sort out any customer issues. My comp plan was a disaster. I essentially reduced the setting of quota to a mathematical formula, and then, foolishly published that formula. The plan was simple enough: to make your targeted earning for the quarter, you needed to sell the amount you sold in the previous quarter plus 20%. How could a mature rep possibly add 20% each quarter? I don't think I could have devised a worse plan for my best reps. They all thanked me by resigning within three months. I had never put myself in their shoes and didn't spend more than a minute on the plan. I should've read this book.

An additional side effect of a good plan that retains great reps is that it usually does not retain poor reps. If you have a low base salary, a rep who isn't selling, can't afford to continue working at your company, at least not in sales. He will find another position probably with a company with a higher base and a quota plan, hopefully, with your competitor.

5. Pays More Per Dollar Sold to Those Who Sell More

Your plan should pay an increasing percentage per dollar sold. For example, the plan at Minicomputer Corp (before it was ruined) paid 1% on sales up to $500,000, 2% to $750,000, and

3% for anything over $750,000. The best reps got paid more per dollar sold (3%) than the mediocre ones (1% or 2%). This wasn't just a reward for successful reps; it was a motivator for unsuccessful reps. They worked harder, knowing their income could rise exponentially with each new sale.

The beauty is that even with increasing commission percentages, your best reps are still cheaper than your mediocre ones. Yes, you pay them more per dollar sold (3% not 1%), but since they have only one base salary, one office expense, and one fifth of a manager, they cost you a lower percentage of revenue. Most CEOs don't know this. It will help you really love your best reps when you realize the person you are handing that $300,000 commission check to is your lowest cost-per-dollar-sold rep. Consider this example with the 1%-2%-3% plan above:

Figure 13.1 Good vs. Great Rep Cost of Sales		
	Good Rep	Great Rep
Sales Revenue	$ 1,000,000	$ 5,000,000
Base Salary	$ 60,000	$ 60,000
Commission:		
1% to $500K	$ 5,000	$ 5,000
2% to $750K	$ 5,000	$ 5,000
3% over $750K	$ 7,500	$ 127,500
Total Compensation	$ 77,500	$ 197,500
% Cost of Sales	7.75%	3.95%

A great rep costs half as much as the good rep. That is very valuable to understand as a CEO. You will not mind paying them in full.

6. Treats Each Dollar of Revenue as a Dollar of Revenue

I know this sounds stupid but it is important to understand.

Many companies don't follow it at all. They pay more for a dollar of new customer revenue than a dollar of current customer revenue, or for selling one product or service instead of another. Putting aside the fact that current customers are actually more valuable than new ones, you want your sales force properly motivated for all opportunities. Your comp plan shouldn't play favorites.

During the heyday of IBM office products, their sales reps had to hit 100% of quota for all product divisions in order to make the 100% club. And if you weren't in the 100% club for three years, you couldn't get promoted. At the time, IBM had easy-to-sell products like Selectric typewriters, medium-to-sell products like copiers, and impossible-to-sell products like dictating machines. So the reps would spend one day per month selling typewriters, three days selling copiers, and the rest of the month desperately trying to sell a single dictating machine. If IBM had treated each dollar of revenue the same, they would have sold 20 to 30 times as many typewriters, 5 to 10 times as many copiers, and no dictating machines. Their skewed comp plan not only hurt sales, it distorted feedback to the marketing, R&D, and planning departments, all of whom continued to invest in dictating equipment since it was "selling well".

At MiniComputer Corp. they didn't pay commissions on service contracts, so I didn't sell any. Seemed fair, but they didn't like it. No reps sold any. When they did institute commissions on service contracts, I immediately went to one of my biggest customers and sold 300 service contracts.. Show me your comp plan and I will tell you what your sales rep will be doing, in spite of you wanting them to do something else.

So as to not mislead you on revenue, I am highly in favor of paying commission on margin as well as revenue. Paying on gross margin (price minus direct costs) better aligns the reps' motivation with the companies. He will focus on highly profitable products at the expense of lower margin products. There are a lot of examples of this in coming chapters.

This isn't to say that targeted spiffs (short term specific payments) are a bad thing; they can be very effective as you can see in point 10 below, but they should be short term. You don't want to institutionalize skewed motivations in your plan.

7. Ensures Your Current Customers are Treated Better than New Ones

Before designing your plan, stop and think about what you really want your sales rep to do.? If your answer is land more new customers, you will design a disastrous plan. I believe that for 99% of all companies, whether service companies or product companies, the following should be the priority of the sales comp plan:

1. Do not lose a current customer.

2. Sell more to current customers.

3. Go after new customers.

Your comp plan should reflect these priorities. Caring for existing customers is the most important job of any sales organization, and is far-too-often undervalued by management.

Your current customers keep you in business and are your best source of incremental revenue.

Remember, your current customers are your competitors' new customers. Do you really want your competitor's reps more highly incented to take your existing customers away than your reps are to keep them? Regretfully, most CEOs only want to compensate reps for new business as if old business sells itself.

A sale is not a one-time event; it is a continuous process. Selling a new customer is not very time consuming. Servicing one that buys $5,000,000 per year is a killer. You want your best reps highly motivated to make sure current customers love your company and its products or services.

Many companies transfer responsibility for current customers to another group called Account Executives, Customer Care, or other non-sales names. Subsequent commissions to your sales reps are either cut severely or totally when this happens. The Customer Care group is usually not on commission. This is referred to as the Hunter/Farmer model. Hunters get new customers and farmers service existing customers. If you add support personnel to an account, and you should, do not reduce the customer retention responsibility of your sales rep. You want your reps as motivated to protect that account as your competitor's reps are to steal it from you. More on the Hunter/Farmer structure later.

8. Controls the Cost of Selling

A comp plan should highly motivate your best reps but simultaneously keep the percentage cost of selling in line. Most comp plans that consist of a base salary plus a commission based on revenue or margin do this for you. This is one of the few win-wins in business: pay more, but it costs you less as a percentage of sales.

An example will get this across better. At AsiaSoft, our cost of selling was targeted to be 25% of revenue. Our sales comp plan was $5,000 monthly base plus 6% of margin, so if you sold $2,000,000 margin, you earned $60,000 base per year plus $120,000 commission for a total of $180,000. That is a 9.0% cost of selling. The percentage actually goes down as the revenue or margin per rep goes up. If a rep sold $4,000,000, his compensation would be $300,000 or 7.5% of revenue. Pretty cool.

It is really great to know that huge commission checks actually reduce your percentage cost of selling. And, as an added bonus, they attract and retain talented reps, incent more selling, and thus amortize your fixed sales costs over greater revenue. You can pay them cheerfully.

9. Aligns Rep and Management Motivations

You probably don't want to hear this, but when you design your comp plan, it needs to include all levels of sales management from VP of Sales to Regional Sales Director to Sales Rep. The good news is that you can use essentially the same plan, modifying only the bases and the percentage commissions.

This also ensures everyone is on the same page. You don't want your sales managers pulling in a different direction than your reps, or your VP of Sales conflicting with your mangers.

Once at Minicomputer Corp. my branch manager was begging me to delay shipment of a big order so it hit next year. He was on a percentage of quota plan, and, if I shipped, he would get a bigger quota the following year. I was on an increasing percentage of revenue plan and, at that point of the year, I was earning 3% which would revert to 1% at the start of next year. I shipped it.

Be sure to align sales reps with each other, too. This sounds crazy, but you want your reps incented to collaborate. For example, you should pay a phone rep when he refers a prospect to an outside enterprise rep and the sale closes. In that case, AsiaSoft pays double commission. Before we paid double commissions, phone sales reps were not referring business to the enterprise reps. Once an incentive to cooperate was added, phone reps almost referred too many leads. We set the cut off on phone sales dual commissions to one year after the referral, so we didn't pay dual commissions forever.

I'm against splitting commissions because it usually incents the wrong action. For example the phone sales reps at Asia Soft were paid 10% and the outside reps were paid 6%. If instead of double commissions, where both the phone rep and the outside rep were paid their full commission, we had "split" the commission paying the phone rep 6% and the outside rep 4%, the phone reps wouldn't have referred any leads thinking they would close it themselves and earn the full 10%.

Align departments with each other, too. Incent your disparate departments, e.g. web and retail, to collaborate for maximum company sales, not compete for their parochial interests. This is usually achieved by paying a referral fee or a double commission or the like.

One example of alignment gone wrong was a catalog company that tested a retail store in Palo Alto, near their company headquarters. The catalog division didn't get any credit for store sales and the store didn't get any credit for catalog sales. As you could guess, store sales spiked whenever a new catalog was mailed. Since sales per catalog mailed in Palo Alto were the lowest in the nation, due to customers driving into the retail store, the catalog manager stopped mailing catalogs to Palo Alto. The store started to fail until the COO discovered this highly distorted motivation. He then wisely gave the catalog division credit for store sales and vice versa. Now the store is putting a catalog in every purchase and collecting customer names for the mailing list and the catalog manager has upped the mailings to Palo Alto. The company now has hundreds of successful stores combined with a strong catalog.

10. Gives your Reps and Managers Incremental Reasons to Hustle

Even with a great sales comp plan, you can add 20-30% to your reps' revenue by giving them more reasons to hustle in the short term. Depending on the selling cycle, these motivators can take different forms. You can add a $500 spiff (special one-time payment for a specific goal) for the fifth and tenth sale each month. You can have a contest for the most sales of a new product this quarter (keep the time short so you don't run into the IBM dictating machine problem). You can even run a spiff for new Fortune 500 customers.

One of the main reasons I like short-term kickers, aside from the revenue boost of course, is they remind management that sales reps are very important. You should publish weekly or monthly "Kickers" reports to give management a chance to recognize the achievements of many reps, many times per year.

Protecting your Great Comp Plan

Protecting your comp plan is as important as developing it. In time, even a great plan, perhaps especially a great plan, will face the inevitable barrage of meddlers who share a dislike of sales reps and their perceived high compensation. You have to nip these changes in the bud—they never end well. I know; I've seen it, and at times been a victim of all manner of disastrous comp plan changes. Don't let it happen to your company. Once you have a great plan, it's critical that you—the CEO—protect it, especially from HR and Finance.

At AsiaSoft where we had a great comp plan, I noticed that the end-of-quarter sales spike had gone away. When the CEO checked, the HR department had removed the quarterly commission accelerator, without the knowledge or approval of the CEO. No reason given, just removed it. Envy, maybe?

One of the best examples of protecting a good situation was a story told to me by one of my heroes, David Ogilvy, founder of Ogilvy and Mather Advertising. I had the pleasure of spending an evening with him at his chateau in France. It was a humbling experience I still treasure. Among many great stories interspersed with great wine, David told me this one:

> Shell Oil was our biggest account in the New York office when their CEO invited me to go Marlin

fishing in Florida. I don't especially like fishing but when the CEO of your largest account calls, you go. I knew the purpose of the outing was to renegotiate our fees, so I reviewed the account in detail. Luckily, the campaign was working extremely well.

The second day fishing, after two glasses of a superb French wine, the CEO said, "David, how many people do you have assigned to Shell's account?"

I knew the answer. "Three hundred and six," I replied.

He swallowed, incredulous. "David, you haven't changed the campaign in three years. What do all those people do?"

"They keep your people from changing a highly successful campaign."

That was it. He understood my answer, agreed with it, and our fees remained intact.

You won't have 306 people to protect your comp plan, just you. It's your job to stop changes unless they increase the reps' motivation and thus increase your company's growth. Once you commit to a plan, it should be changed only after much discussion, and that discussion should involve your key sales reps, sales managers and, hopefully, exclude your CFO and VP of HR.

Just as a rule of thumb, CFOs should be kept far away from

comp plans, both during development and any subsequent changes. I've never seen a CFO-derived plan that didn't destroy motivation for the reps. Don't get me wrong; I love CFOs. They've saved me tons on taxes, cut my costs, and found new and better ways of financing my business. But keep them away from the sales comp plan. They should be involved in the financial model of the company as a whole: engineering 8%, admin 5% and so on, but once set, let the sales department and the CEO develop a motivational comp plan.

The reps, on the other hand, should be involved. It's their life and career. No modifications to the plan should come as a surprise to them. Changing the comp plan is very threatening to reps. They've typically never seen a sales comp plan change for the better from their perspective. So if you are going to change it, do it quickly; do it carefully; and do it openly. During the change period, reps aren't selling. They're worrying, polishing their résumés, and surfing LinkedIn. It is a dangerous time for your company.

The sales comp plan is a critical strategic element of your business, and you can create a dynamite one by following the guidelines above and the more detailed examples in the next chapters. And remember to achieve your revenue targets consistently, you need a combination of a great plan and a continually increasing number of sales reps. The plan can't do it alone, nor can a bevy of reps sell much with a bad plan.

CHAPTER 14

Two Failed Comp Plans

This chapter probably describes your current sales comp plan. Sorry. The reason for failure is not only built into your comp plan, but usually built into the CEO's and the entire company's attitude toward sales reps. So this chapter will be very important since it shows you what not to do.

Failed comp plan features that cause the most issues are:

a) Focusing on new customers at the expense of keeping current customers,

b) Resetting the comp plan each year, thus penalizing your best sales reps, and

c) Negotiating or rationalizing not paying full commission after the sale is made.

The most popular failed comp plan is the one that is most prevalent, the one I call the Treadmill Plan.

1. The Treadmill Plan

The Treadmill Plan is a slow disaster. It drives your best sales reps out of your company and into your competitor's arms. You retain your less ambitious sales reps who produce a moderate amount of revenue, and your CFO will be pleased because no rep will earn more than he. It has appeal to all but great sales reps.

Figure 14.1 Sisyphus probably invented the Treadmill Sales Comp Plan.

I have named this plan the "Treadmill" due to its Sisyphus nature. You have your sales reps on an annual treadmill, whereby, they have to run faster and faster each year until they just can't anymore. The plan is disguised many ways, but the basics are that the sales territory quota gets set every year along with a level of compensation for reaching that quota. Say I have a quota of $3,000,000 in revenue to meet and for that I get $150,000 in annual compensation, comprised of $60,000 in base and $90,000 in commission (3%). If I sell only $2,000,000 I would earn $120,000. If I sell $5,000,000 I would earn $210,000. Sounds like an okay plan: no cap on commissions, goals commensurate with territory potential, and pay for performance.

So what's the problem? One problem is the annual adversarial setting of quota. The sales rep and his sales manager argue at length about the territory's potential. This argument detracts from selling time, and it is usually worth more for the sales rep to win this argument than it is to sell more. It leaves a bad taste in everyone's mouth. This is not conducive to a motivational selling environment.

A second problem is a multiyear sale. If you sell a three year contract, you don't get paid in years 2 and 3 since the company will just build those sales into your quota.

The worst aspect of this plan is the fact that your best sales reps get royally screwed. They get paid significantly less per dollar sold. This eventually forces your star sales reps to go to your competitor, which is a double whammy. You not only lose the sale but your competitor gets it.

Your plan should be designed to keep your sales reps at your company for life. Once they climb the sales S-Curve, they should consistently be paid too much money, which will still be below the percent cost of sales of an average rep. At one company, the rep earned 5X the CEO and the CEO loved it. Of course the CEO owned 20% of the company and, as a result of the rep, his stock was greatly appreciating.

Take this Treadmill Test Yourself

To really understand the Treadmill, consider the performance of the following four sales reps all hired at the same time:

Figure 14.2 Four Reps Revenue Per Year				
	Rep 1	Rep 2	Rep 3	Rep 4
Year 1	$200,000	$300,000	$300,000	$400,000
Year 2	$400,000	$1,500,000	$1,500,000	$1,500,000
Year 3	$500,000	$3,000,000	$1,500,000	$800,000
Next Year's Quota	?	?	?	?

What is the sales quota you or your sales manager assigns next year? Fill it in. In spite of the concept that quotas are assigned according to the territory's sales potential, they are almost always assigned based on last year's revenue and growth rate. I would contend that the four sales reps illustrated above would be assigned the quotas similar to the ones below:

Figure 14.3 Treadmill Plan Quota Assignments				
	Rep 1	Rep 2	Rep 3	Rep 4
Next Year's Quota	$600,000	$4,500,000	$2,000,000	$1,200,000

If we have the comp plan consisting of a $60,000 base salary and $90,000 targeted commission for 100% quota performance, your reps would earn the following for the actual "Next Year's Revenue" listed in line 3, below:

Figure 14.4 Treadmill Plan Actual Compensation Paid				
	Rep 1	Rep 2	Rep 3	Rep 4
Next Year's Quota	$600,000	$4,500,000	$2,000,000	$1,200,000
Target Income on Quota	$150,000	$150,000	$150,000	$150,000
Next Year's Revenue	$800,000	$3,000,000	$2,500,000	$1,500,000
Base	$60,000	$60,000	$60,000	$60,000
Commission	$120,000	$75,000	$112,500	$112,500
Total Compensation	$190,000	$120,000	$172,500	$172,500
% of Sales	24.00%	4.00%	6.90%	11.50%

Do you really think that rep #2 is going to stick around? She sold $3,000,000, $500,000 more than any other rep, but was paid the least. She was only 67% of quota? Can she be considered for promotion even though she was only 67% of goal? Can she be invited to the 100% club meeting in Cabo San Lucas? Rep 4 has figured out the system, she holds orders at the end of every other year and thus earns more than if her revenue grew smoothly.

Look at your percent cost of sales. Your best rep is costing only 4.0% of revenue while your lowest revenue rep is costing you 24% of revenue. If you paid your best rep $200,000, she would still only cost you 6.7% of revenue. This is the number to focus on, not how much more the best rep makes than the CEO, or the CFO. Concentrate on the percentage cost of selling instead of the dollars actually paid.

Treadmill plans are rampant. To add insult to injury, management sometimes renegotiates after the fact. When a sale is made, the company gets paid; the investors get paid; the CFO gets paid; but the rep that brought the resources to bear to cause the order only gets paid partially. This is a sure way to tell your entire sales force that you don't value them. It will lead to an exodus. And don't think the rep that didn't receive full commission won't tell. Sales people talk, that's what they do best.

In the coming chapters you'll see examples of disguised treadmill plans such as the one that almost caused the entire seven-person sales force to resign (we stopped it after only one resignation) and another that destroyed the best sales force in the minicomputer industry in six months. The company never recovered.

Now let's grade the Treadmill Plan based on the criteria in Chapter 13:

Figure 14.5 Treadmill Plan Scoring Score	Score
1. Provides predictable, reliable commissions.	No
2. Motivates reps to invest in their territory across years.	No
3. Has uncapped commissions.	No
4. Retains your great reps.	No
5. Pays more per dollar sold to those who sell more.	No
6. Treats each dollar of revenue as a dollar of revenue.	No
7. Ensures current customers are treated better than new ones.	No
8. Controls the cost of selling.	Yes
9. Aligns rep and management motivations.	No
10. Gives your reps and managers incremental reasons to hustle.	No
Results: 1 of 10	

A clear failure.

2. The "No Stars" Plan

The No Stars Plan will shock you, but it exists in some companies. It was the plan in effect at Palo Alto Electronics in the early days of the electronics industry. It was the reason I did not go into sales at Palo Alto Electronics and went to a competitor instead. At the time, most of Palo Alto Electronics revenue came from electronic instrument sales. I include it because it is so obviously wrong, yet it was used for years and Palo Alto Electronics continued to grow because they did most other things right, especially hiring at least 30% more sales reps each year.

The plan was simple: it paid 100% of projected sales rep income for 100% of projected sales from the rep's territory, identical to the Treadmill Plan above. What could be fairer? The projected income was management's estimate of what the territory should produce. It was estimated based upon skill, seniority, and other factors that are used in non-selling jobs. This enabled someone from the factory to move into sales without a first year decrease in compensation. It also enabled Palo Alto Electronics to poach other company's reps because they had flexibility in setting the targeted income individually. They tended not to do this, but rather chose to grow their own sales reps.

The projected sales from a territory was negotiated between the rep and his manager. It theoretically was based upon market potential, new companies in his geographical territory, new government contracts awarded to his clients, and so on. In reality, it was set based upon his sales last year in the territory. The formula was last year's revenue plus 20% to 30%, depending upon how much your boss liked you.

The biggest flaw was that the compensation was capped at 120% of projected income. After achieving 120% of target revenue, you received no more compensation, thus the "No Stars" title. Before you go nuts, you have to understand the Palo Alto Electronics philosophy at the time. Throughout the company the mantra was, "All employees are valuable and all work hard, no one is better than the others, and thus all should be compensated similarly." This philosophy carried over to sales compensation. And they were right; few of their sales reps were "Stars". The Stars went to Minicomputer Corp., as I did.

One "Star" did stay at Palo Alto Electronics. He loved the environment, and was getting paid a high salary for the amount of selling effort he put in. He clearly understood the system. He spent at least three months before the annual quota setting moaning about his territory:

"It is dry. I have sucked all the orders out of the companies. They have Palo Alto Electronics instruments stacked to the ceiling in receiving. Three of my clients are moving whole divisions out of my territory," and so on.

This rep's considerable selling efforts were targeted at selling his boss, not his customers. It worked for him, not for Palo Alto Electronics. He would get assigned a high targeted income and a low sales territory target. Upon getting his new quota negotiated, he would open the drawer and pull out purchase order after purchase order that he had been holding back. He would immediately rocket up to 120% of quota again through "lucky orders" and the complaining would commence. I often wonder how much he could have actually sold with a motivational plan.

The No Stars plan actually scores better than the Treadmill since reps can easily calculate their earnings. It is 120% of quota if you are a talented rep.

Conclusion

One real side effect of Treadmill plans is the motivation of your reps not to beat their sales goal by much, if anything. If they do, they just get punished by getting a bigger, harder goal next year. Even worse, what would happen if they closed a large contract shipping over three years? Do you think they would get paid much in years two and three? Of course not, the company would just raise the quota and expect them to sell even more.

Don't be naïve; experienced sales reps know all this. Rookies figure it out in one year. Sales reps who are strong and ambitious hate these plans and leave, or better yet, don't join. Rookies don't mind these plans while they are learning to sell since they are being subsidized by the company. Once they know they can sell, they will find a company that is willing to pay them for their efforts.

When you set up a Treadmill Plan or a No Stars plan, do not get mad at your sales reps for doing things not in the best interest of the company. If you find one of your sales reps holding orders in the drawer for a month to get into a new commission year, if you find he signs no long term contracts, if you find he stops selling the last quarter of the year, don't scream. He is doing exactly what you have told him to do, or more correctly, he is doing exactly what you motivated him to do, which is much more powerful than just telling him.

CHAPTER 15

How to Design a Great Sales Compensation Plan for Products

Designing and protecting a great sales comp plan is one of the major jobs of a CEO. Once you have competitive products, priced correctly, in a large and growing market, it may be the most important job a CEO has. If you have a great sales comp plan and you add too many sales reps, you will consistently and predictably exceed your revenue, profit, and growth forecasts. Life as a CEO will be good.

The Killers and Closers Plan

The salesforce at MiniComputer Corp. was known as "Killers and Closers". It was a compliment.

The comp plan was one of the main reasons that MiniComputer Corp. was able to build an incredibly strong company and strong sales force. During this period, MiniComputer Corp. grew over 100% per year, profitably. The sales force was so strong that at one time there were literally rooms full of unopened purchase orders. We're talking some purchase orders for millions of dollars each that remained unopened for months. The company was adding a "football field" of production capacity each month and still was unable to keep up with demand. Minicomputer Corp was doubling the size of the sales force each year, and the comp plan motivated us to sell tonnage. It was a ball.

MiniComputer Corp's plan paid the lowest base salary but had the highest compensated sales force in the industry. The VP of Sales would brag, "Each sales rep I hire this year, will sell a million dollars next year and four million two years from now." He understood that sales reps caused sales. He understood the S-Curve. He understood how to leverage an engineer's blood, sweat, and tears. He also understood how to design a great sales comp plan, the only problem is that he just didn't protect it. More on that later, first the comp plan:

Base Salary: $16,000 per year (vintage 1972, adjusted for inflation $88,000 in 2012 dollars).

Commission: 1% to $500,000 in revenue per year, 2% to $750,000, and 3% thereafter. Your commission year commenced upon your hire date, so commission years were staggered across the sales force.

This plan has no cap on sales rep earnings, no management of earnings by paying more for new accounts vs. current accounts, no management manipulation of the best reps' pay, no negotiation of quota or compensation each year, and no changes on January 1st. The commissions were paid in full without management intervention. It was wonderful for sales reps, corporate management and stock holders. It also saved immense amounts of management time and conflict.

I know you were expecting much more, but a great comp plan is simple, understandable, and motivational.

Scoring Killer's and Closers

Let's look in detail at how Killers and Closers stack up on the criteria from Chapter 13:

1. Provides Predictable, Reliable Commissions—Yes

It was easy to calculate and there were no "judgment factors". It did not change from year to year, nor was it a function of an arbitrary quota.

I could calculate the commission in my head and did so many times each day, especially during my big year. It was enjoyable.

The plan even paid commission predictably including for orders when someone just called and ordered a computer from my territory with no effort on my part. Why not? The company got paid, the CEO got paid, and the shareholders got paid, why not the sales rep? These "Blue Birds" (unexpected orders) were wonderful, like winning the lottery.

2. One that Motivates Sales Reps to Invest in Their Territory Across Years—Yes

The plan paid an accelerating percentage for more revenue. It paid the best sales reps the most and it enabled a sales rep to make more than the CEO (one rep made 5X the CEO) and it didn't punish the best reps with a higher quota following a great selling year.

Since the Killers and Closers did not pay on quota and the comp plan was the same every year, we were highly motivated to sell like hell. The best accounts were those that repeatedly purchased computers for the coming years, like the CAT scanner manufacturer that built in our computer, or the educational computer company that placed "drill and practice" computers in underprivileged elementary schools by the hundreds, or the CAD design company that built our computers into their system. We would go after these "annuity" accounts knowing we would get paid three years from now at the same rate as now. (Regretfully, that later proved to be wrong.)

3. Has Uncapped Commissions—Yes

A rep can invest in his territory now and reap the benefits next year or even the following year since he knows how he will be paid. No higher quota will kill his commission check.

4. Retains Your Great Reps—Yes

As we worked our way up the S-Curve, we started to make serious money. No way would we even consider leaving Minicomputer Corp. Those of us who closed orders from companies that built our computer into their products were especially locked in. I had three, each buying over $1 million and growing every year. My plan really motivated me to make sure their computers shipped on time and were serviced on time, and that they had advance knowledge of new products.

Under the Killers and Closers plan your best reps get paid the most for each dollar of revenue they deliver. They are uncapped, don't have to worry about increased quotas, and can really invest in their territories even across years.

Non-selling reps starve. They join competitors with higher bases and quota-based compensation. Having your worst reps join a competitor is a double win. You retain the best sales reps, and they get the worst ones. Life is good.

5. Pays More Per Dollar Sold to Those Who Sell More—Yes

Since I had climbed the commission rate ladder, I was getting 3% per dollar sold. Reps selling less were getting only 1% or 2%. Even better, I knew that next year I would get into 3% money quickly since I had three customers shipping $400,000 of my computers per month. It would only take me two months to be back into 3% money.

6. Treats Each Dollar of Revenue as a Dollar of Revenue—Yes

It did not matter if I sold a current customer, a new customer, or a service contract. I got paid and the company got paid.

One exception to this rule would be if your reps had pricing discretion. In that case I would pay commission on margin and not top line revenue. This motivates the reps to sell a higher price instead of caving. I contend you are still treating a dollar of revenue as a dollar of revenue; it's just a dollar of margin revenue.

7. Ensures Current Customers are Treated Better than New Ones—Yes

Since I was paid the same for existing customers' revenue and it was easier to get additional orders from my current customers, that is where I spent my time. My first year, I had no customers, so I closed 19 new ones. My second year, I closed six new customers since I was busy helping my prior 19 customers get their systems operating. And in my third year, I was in full harvest mode with my three major customers each shipping hundreds of computers per year. My current customers were well taken care of.

8. One that Controls the Cost of Selling—Yes

In spades.

The cost of the direct compensation to sales reps is fixed at just above 3%. If a rep sold a million dollars, the cost of the rep was $31,000: $16,000 base plus $5,000 (1% to $500,000) plus $10,000 (2% between $500,000 and $1,000,000) for a total of $31,000 or 3.1% of revenue.

If you sold $4,000,000, the cost of the direct compensation was still fixed at just above 3%: $16,000 base plus $5,000 (1% to $500,000) plus $10,000 (2% between $500,000 and $1,000,000), plus $90,000 for a total of $121,000 or just a hair above 3%.

This is a very important point: Even though the company is paying the sales rep selling four million dollars of revenue $121,000 ($500,000 in 2012 dollars), this rep costs the company the same percentage of revenue as a rep selling one-fourth as much.

A final point: By staggering the compensation years, namely starting the 1%, 2% and 3% ramps from the date of hire, the monthly percentage cost of selling stays at slightly below 3%, since some reps are into 3% money, while others are reset to 1% because their year recently rolled around. This makes budgeting easy and actual sales expenses predictable. And staggering the reps' commission years avoids all your great sales reps from joining forces and negotiating a group comp package on January 1st.

9. Aligns Rep and Management Motivations—Yes

No quota, no negotiation, no conflict with management.

10. Gives your Reps and Managers Incremental Reasons to Hustle—Yes

Quarterly sales contests did this. They weren't a part of the plan per se but were expected and were fun. One would focus on new customers at Fortune 500 companies. Another would pay a spiff for selling a new product. Another contest would move systems that were overstocked and so on.

The real value of these contests was that they gave management more opportunities to recognize achievement.

Figure 15.1 Killers and Closers Scoring Score	Score
1. Provides predictable, reliable commissions.	Yes
2. Motivates reps to invest in their territory across years.	Yes
3. Has uncapped commissions.	Yes
4. Retains your great reps.	Yes
5. Pays more per dollar sold to those who sell more.	Yes
6. Treats each dollar of revenue as a dollar of revenue.	Yes
7. Ensures current customers are treated better than new ones.	Yes
8. Controls the cost of selling.	Yes
9. Aligns rep and management motivations.	Yes
10. Gives your reps and managers incremental reasons to hustle.	Yes
Results: 10 of 10	

Overall Killers and Closers is a great plan. You would do well to pattern yours after it.

With the Killers and Closers plan, the sales rep was in control of his or her own destiny. If he landed a three year contract, he expected to get compensated, and he did. Minicomputer Corp. paid me every dollar the plan required, why wouldn't they? I was the cheapest sales rep they had. In 1975, I earned $252,000 ($1,350,000 in 2012 dollars) in commission for almost $10 million ($50 million in 2012 dollars) in revenue (2.5% of sales), and they not only paid it, they bragged about it. Think about that. What effect do you think handing one of your sales reps a $1,350,000 check would have on the other sales reps? What effect did paying me have on their ability to hire new sales reps? You can hear the interview now, "One of our salesmen earned five times more than the CEO."

CHAPTER 16

How to Design a Great Compensation Plan for Services

"If this is your comp plan, you will lose all your sales reps in the next sixty days."

That was my statement when I read the new comp plan at ATM Cash, $200 million service company. When I said this to the CEO, he turned white and murmured, "My second best sales rep resigned last night. What should I do?"

I had been asked to analyze the stalled sales problem by one of the company's private equity investors. ATM Cash placed and serviced ATMs and other cash access systems. They had a large market share, but their growth had stalled. The CEO, who was very talented, was frustrated they weren't getting new business. So, in a move I'm sure seemed eminently logical to him, he changed the sales comp plan to only pay for new customers and not the maintenance or growth of current customers. This would incent new business, he reasoned, and besides, he'd already paid his reps for selling their current customers.

It was a disaster in the making. CEOs too often believe selling is a one-time event and that current customers take no selling time or effort. They also tend to undervalue sales reps in general, making CEOs willing, if not eager, to slash comp plans. ATM Cash's CEO had acted on his misconceptions: that existing business maintains itself, that reps exist solely to bring in new customers, and worst of all, that current customers are less important than new ones.

His changes were even more egregious because the company had a large market share including all the major locations. For one thing, this meant new business could only come from smaller remote locations, like Dubuque, Iowa. "Do you really want a larger multi-location chain ignored while your best sales rep flies to Dubuque, Iowa?" I asked. Moreover, ATM Cash's dominant market share made it particularly tied to its existing customers. Remember, from your competitors' view, all your current customers are their potential new customers. So I asked the CEO, "What are your competitors paying their reps to take all this business away from you? Do you want their sales reps more motivated to steal this account than yours are to keep it?"

To his credit, the CEO considered the questions quickly. ATM Cash had seven sales reps, well, really six since one just resigned. The best one handled six of the ten biggest chains, for which he, going forward, would be paid next to nothing. The CEO began to see my point. Lifting his head from the desk, he asked, "What do I do?" I suggested. "Send an email saying that you're going back to the former plan, a good plan that grew them to $200 million in very profitable revenue, and tell them you hired a sales-rep-friendly consultant."

I've seen too many companies stumble, even fail, because they undervalued their own existing customers. Fortunately, ATM Cash would not be one of them.

Why Service Company Plans Get Screwed Up

Most CEOs think their company or industry is unique, and it is in many ways, but it also has the same underlying motivations. That is why hiring tons of sales reps and motivating them with a great comp plan works for most, if not all, industries. I find service industries, especially ones that sell on an annuity basis like placing ATMs in stores on a three year contract, selling a five-year buying group service contract, or selling social network support services, can really be leveraged by adding sales reps.

My experience is that service company sales comp plans are often the most screwed up, especially those industries that sell multiyear contracts. The reason these companies can survive and continue to grow slowly is that annuity revenue keeps coming in for a long period of time even if the comp plan isn't ideal and their best sales reps have been forced out of the company. As you lose your top sales reps and keep the mediocre ones, revenue from the former top reps continues for years after they have departed, which distorts results.

Incent Your Sales Reps to Love Their Current Customers

Current customers are more valuable than potential new customers. Losing a major customer is devastating, and losing expected revenue is far worse than not getting new revenue. Yet many companies seem to think sales reps exist primarily or solely to get new customers.

A good comp plan should motivate reps to serve current customers first and then new customers. Re-signing a current customer is almost always cheaper and thus more profitable than landing a new one, yet companies are reluctant to pay their reps much commission for doing it. If it's more profitable, arguably you could pay more, not less.

Keys to Service Comp Plan Design

Service comp plans can have some compensation tilt toward new customer acquisition or renewal of current customers, but the key is to also pay for retaining your current customers. Think of being a sales rep for an annuity revenue firm. You want to be highly motivated to invest your time and efforts over the long term. Here is what you are thinking, "A new customer will pay me for the next five years. Now, if I get one new customer per month for the next three years…" Design your plan to keep that dream alive and to lock in both customers and your top sales reps.

What I Learned from Life Insurance Comp Plans

I was intrigued as a kid growing up in small town Ohio as to why the life insurance rep seemed to have more money than the doctors and lawyers. His son was my age. They had a beautiful home. His dad was always free to coach little league, and they gave a substantial amount to the church (the church published contributions by donor for all to see, a cruel, but effective technique). It still amazes me that I was into comp plans and motivation at ten years old, maybe it was just envy.

I had a chance to quiz my friend's dad when I was in high school. I found out he received a commission upon selling a new insurance policy plus a residual for maintaining previously-sold policies. After ten years as an independent insurance rep, he had thousands of policies in place and, even if he didn't sell one more policy, he could live very comfortably, at least until his clients died. Gruesome concept.

Had the plan not paid for maintaining previously sold customers, he would have moved all his clients over to a new company every few years, capturing a second, third, and fourth "new customer" commission. With a residual, he was extremely motivated to sell early and often, and, once sold, to never lose or transfer a customer.

The reason that life insurance companies don't screw up their comp plans, while most other industries do, is that their agents are independent and can easily change from one company to another. In fact, agents usually sell for two or three insurance providers, just to keep these insurance companies off guard. I contend the insurance companies had no choice but to be smart about compensation.

Designing an ATM Cash Comp Plan

The plan the CEO and I designed for ATM Cash was patterned after the insurance company plan above. It paid as well for renewal of an existing client as it did for adding a new customer.

The key was to pay an ongoing retention commission to keep current customers protected from competition, exactly like an insurance company did.

Because pricing was negotiable, we paid reps more for high margin business and we paid more for longer-term contracts. The new plan worked spectacularly well.

Before the plan was put in place, over 90% of their customers were on month-to-month contracts. This was best for the reps in the short term, because the customer often didn't realize their contact had expired. Only when a competitive sales rep called on the customer did the customer even check. Once competition was involved, the margin would crater, and we risked losing the entire account. Our competition lived off our previously stupid comp plan.

After only six months on our new comp plan, most of the top ten customers were on five year contracts and about 70% of all customers were on five year contracts. Revenue and margins were now very predictable, only the volume of ATM transactions varied.

An unexpected side effect was the fact that our two biggest competitors began having serious financial and growth problems. I should have predicted this, but I didn't. Their sales reps had nowhere to hunt. Our customers were now placed off limits by our five year contract. Competitors would have to wait five years to have a shot at unhooking even one of them.

Can you believe an effective sales comp plan can be this strategic? This is why I emphasize: Your job as CEO is to design and protect your sales reps' comp plan! These are your foot soldiers; give them the motivation and weapons to win their unfair share of new business and to protect your conquered territory.

Here Are the Details of the ATM Cash Plan

Ongoing Commissions: monthly commissions are paid for all products and services revenue from current customers. After they close a lot of customers, this ongoing commission adds up and locks the great reps firmly to your company:

Figure 16.1 ATM Cash Compensation Plan					
Margin		Length of Contract			
From	To	Month to Month	1 Year	3 Year	5 Year
20%	25%	3%	5%	7%	10%
26%	30%	4%	6%	8%	11%
31%	35%	5%	7%	9%	12%
36%	40%	6%	8%	10%	13%
41%	99%	7%	9%	11%	15%

As you can see the cost of selling for this program is way below the 30% of gross margin target, topping out at 15%. Added to this ongoing commission is the new product/customer renewal commission, on next page.

As an aside, the sales rep managers were on an identical plan getting paid 30% of the total commission while the rep received 70%. If a manager had five good reps working for him, he would receive 30% times five or 1.5 times as much as his reps. This enabled us to promote selling reps into management positions.

New Product/Customer/Renewal Bonus: A one-year commission bonus is paid for selling an additional product into an existing account, adding a new customer, or renewing an existing customer. A new product/customer is defined as a product or customer that hasn't purchased from the company in the prior 36 months.

Figure 16.2 New Product/Customer/Renewal Bonus (% of Margin)						
Margin		Length of Contract				
From	To	1 Year	2 Year	3 Year	4 Year	5 Year
20%	25%	0.09%	0.20%	0.46%	1.03%	2.31%
26%	30%	0.12%	0.27%	0.61%	1.37%	3.08%
31%	35%	0.15%	0.34%	0.76%	1.71%	3.84%
36%	99%	0.18%	0.41%	0.91%	2.05%	4.61%

Shingling – Your Secret Weapon

A secret weapon for annuity service comp plans is "Shingling". This is the technique of motivating both your sales reps and your existing customers to never let a contract expire, or even come close to expiring. An example is BuyingService Group. At BuyingService they sold a five year contract. We designed a plan whereby if a rep closed an early renewal (two years prior to the expiration date of the contract), they earned a higher commission than if the contract was one year or less from expiring, and much higher than if it had actually expired.

The concept of Shingling (my name since it has overlapped contracts like shingles on a roof) needs to be combined with a marketing offer that motivates the customer as well, not just the sales rep. For example, at ATM Cash we had a set of marketing reports that we priced at $500 per month or $6,000 per year. At these prices, we sold very few reports, but they were a great tool to get a customer to renew his contract early. At the three anniversary of their contract, we would offer the reports free for the next five years if they would extend the contract for an additional five years (a three year extension). That worked. No new contract terms negotiation, no competitive bidding, and no margin erosion all in exchange for reports that cost us nothing. And the competitors' sales reps were closed out for five more years.

If you want to see the masters of this approach, look at mobile phone companies. Their contract extends another two years if you change one term or reduce or add one service. If your contract is about to expire, they offer you a "free" phone costing them up to $800. They understand the value of retaining current customers well.

Automatic Renewal – the Ultimate Shingling

My post-college roommate had a direct mail company selling a guide for checking IDs (for bars, rental car agencies, police forces, etc.). He did an annual mailing that resulted in a good stream of orders. One day I asked him why he didn't sell a three year or five year subscription instead of having to convince his customers to buy each year. He just hadn't thought of it. When he tried it, it worked well. Most orders were for three years with a smattering of five years. His profits skyrocketed. Then he one-upped me and came up with the "Auto Renewal". The subscription continued until cancelled. It worked extremely well. Soon he moved out of our apartment since automatic renewal enabled him to purchase a great new home.

At ATM Cash they added a term to the five-year contract that stated, "If this contract is not cancelled 90 days prior to expiration, it auto renews for an additional five years." I suspect it will really work. It hasn't been five years yet, so I can't tell. They theorized that nobody would remember to cancel and that the person signing the contract would either be gone or promoted by the time the fifth anniversary came up. It seems a bit shady, I prefer motivating customers to renew willingly.

Scoring ATM Cash's Comp Plan

Figure 16.3 ATMService Plan Scoring	Score
1. Provides predictable, reliable commissions.	Yes
2. Motivates reps to invest in their territory across years.	Yes
3. Has uncapped commissions.	Yes
4. Retains your great reps.	Yes
5. Pays more per dollar sold to those who sell more.	Yes
6. Treats each dollar of revenue as a dollar of revenue.	Yes
7. Ensures current customers are treated better than new ones.	Yes
8. Controls the cost of selling.	Yes
9. Aligns rep and management motivations.	Yes
10. Gives your reps and managers incremental reasons to hustle.	Via Contests
Results: 10 of 10	

Buying Services Comp Plan

When I began consulting for Buying Services they had five sales reps with a treadmill plan (target reset annually, completely managing sales rep income and driving the top reps out of the company). The company wasn't growing. This is a very typical scenario for a sales rep constrained company with a non-motivational comp plan.

By now you should be able to predict the plan I put in place: promote the current sales reps to sales managers, add 25 new sales reps reporting to them, institute a multi-year motivational comp plan, then align the sales managers' comp plans with the reps' plan, and duck.

The plan consisted of five parts:

1. Base—Very conservative $3,000/mo.

2. Recurring Commission—Modest but highly motivational especially for a rep that sold successfully for the company for two years having closed 125+ new customers (five per month over two years) during that period. 125 customers times modest commission equals a great base of earnings.

3. Renewal Commission—Borrowed from ATM Cash. We paid well both for closing a new customer and for renewing a current customer. The renewal commission was about 80% of the new customer commission. It should have been higher.

4. New Member Commission—Easy; it paid for each new member. Due to the fact that most CEOs only want to pay for new members, this one paid well. I had to hack it back down repeatedly so I still had some money to pay for renewals and residuals.

5. Monthly Accelerators—The most fun for the sales managers. We paid a bonus each month for any rep over five new customers or renewals that month, a bigger bonus for more than ten. We also had a quarterly cumulative bonus for new accounts and renewals. It paid for landing 10 new accounts/renewals in the first quarter, raised to 25 the 2nd quarter, 40 the 3rd and 50 for the full commission year. This really got our 1st half off to a roaring start. If a rep got 15 new or renewals in the first quarter, he was in very good shape to earn all the bonuses.

The reason it was fun for the managers is that they were on a similar bonus structure. If a rep was close to earning his bonus, the manager would call and say: "Can I help? You only need three more new customers in the next month to hit your and my bonus. I'll come to town and we'll each make three calls per day and one in the evening." The reps now welcomed the help.

Figure 16.4 Buying Group Plan Scoring	Score
1. Provides predictable, reliable commissions.	Yes
2. Motivates reps to invest in their territory across years.	Yes
3. Has uncapped commissions.	Yes
4. Retains your great reps.	Yes
5. Pays more per dollar sold to those who sell more.	Yes
6. Treats each dollar of revenue as a dollar of revenue.	Yes
7. Ensures current customers are treated better than new ones.	Yes
8. Controls the cost of selling.	Yes
9. Aligns rep and management motivations.	Yes
10. Gives your reps and managers incremental reasons to hustle.	Via Contests
Results: 10 of 10	

Social Media Marketing

Social Media Marketing sold via a 100% telephone sales force. Eventually, they would be ready to add enterprise reps but it was early in the company's history. They had one office with seven sales reps in Miami. If you plotted their sales as a function of zip code, most customers were in Florida. As you suspect by now, I recommended multiple sales offices with five reps each, the number manageable by one sales manager.

Since all customers paid essentially the same fee each month, it was easier to design a plan that dealt in the number of new customer and number of renewals (this was not auto renewal). This was a startup so all customers were new, but we designed renewals into the plan from the start so the reps could see their commissions growing cumulatively in the future.

Again the plan was simple: 100% of the first month's payment from the customer as the new customer commission, plus a 5% per month residual, plus some exciting monthly accelerators. They had monthly accelerators, not quarterly or annual ones, since they were a quick close type of service: one call to schedule a demo and one call to close or move on.

This company was located in a college town so you could hire reps at a very low base, namely $2,000 per month. This enabled them to pay aggressive commissions to their top performing reps. The problem was that it took rookies two to three months to get up to speed. To supplement their income and to recognize their achievement we instituted a $500 first sale bonus, a $1,000 fifth sale bonus, and a $1,000 tenth sale bonus. The bonuses expired at the end of month three. This enabled us to cheer their progress and supplement their income without increasing their base. It worked well.

A second point about this company: They were reluctant to establish remote sales offices, as are most corporate managements. With adequate pressure, they put in their first remote office and, in the first month of its operation, it surpassed their corporate sales office in revenue per rep. That, in spite of the fact that all the reps were rookies. Remote sales offices work better than ones near the home office since all the remote offices have to do is sell without any interruptions. At corporate there is more to do, more people to talk to, and more questions to answer from management and marketing. I love pure sales offices.

A New Car

Management of Social Media Marketing heard me tell the story of the Asian board meeting and my comment, "Not only should you pay the $300,000 commission owed, but you should give the rep a new car as a bonus." Management was young and really loved the concept, so they implemented it. Their $2,000 per month reps could earn a new car the second year at the company. If any sold 60 new/renewal customers, the company would lease them a car for the following year. It would only cost the company $200 per month. You could not believe the excitement. Everybody was picking out colors, models, and options. We did have to remind the reps that they had to get back on the phones to real customers and exit the car companies' web sites if they really wanted to earn the car.

Figure 16.5 Social Media Marketing Scoring	Score
1. Provides predictable, reliable commissions.	Yes
2. Motivates reps to invest in their territory across years.	Yes
3. Has uncapped commissions.	Yes
4. Retains your great reps.	Yes
5. Pays more per dollar sold to those who sell more.	Yes
6. Treats each dollar of revenue as a dollar of revenue.	Yes
7. Ensures current customers are treated better than new ones.	Yes
8. Controls the cost of selling.	Yes
9. Aligns rep and management motivations.	Yes
10. Gives your reps and managers incremental reasons to hustle.	Via Contests
Results: 10 of 10	

Why Service Companies Don't Have Motivational Comp Plans

Great sales comp plans for service companies are hard to sell to CEOs because once a customer is closed, many people at corporate–other than the rep–work hard servicing that company. It seems unfair that the reps should get a retention bonus and not the people producing the services themselves. CEOs of services companies, believe that once a customer is closed, they do not need the sales rep any more.

I have failed at selling my concepts to many service company CEOs. They can follow the logic and follow the math, but it just doesn't feel right to them. They are usually CEOs who are brought into an existing company and are very politically aware. They do not want to change anything, just carry on earning their $300,000 per year salary and wait to cash in their stock option. I am not blaming them; I am blaming their Boards for not pushing them for more growth through a motivational CEO comp plan.

I am still bothered by a large successful healthcare service company I was asked to help. I failed. They sold a cloud-based service to the health industry. It cost them close to zero to add a new customer; all the software was done. To add insult to injury, a new customer for them produced $5 million in first-year revenue minimum. What a great business! It was an especially great one to add sales reps.

The company had five, and only five sales reps, on a treadmill plan. All sales reps were comfortable, all were happy, all were well paid ($200,000 per year), and no boats would be rocked. It killed me. Needless to say the company was not growing when it could have exploded in revenue. The company was doing $450 million in revenue and had not grown for three years. I predict it will be doing $450 million per year ten years from now unless Obamacare kills them.

The CEO said sales reps were too expensive, $200,000 per year. My retort was, "If you hired 20 new reps and paid them $200,000 per year, and one, only one, closed a single order in the first 12 months, you would make an extra $1,000,000 profit." He had not done the calculation: 20 reps times $200,000 per rep = $4,000,000 cost. One new customer yielded $5,000,000 per year revenue and margin. And that doesn't count the fact that you now have 20 reps on board, trained, and ready to close a couple new accounts each the following year. He asked me to go–my bedside manner leaves a little to be desired when I see an opportunity as big as this one. Here is how Health Services Plan scored:

Figure 16.6 HealthServices Plan Scoring	Score
1. Provides predictable, reliable commissions.	No
2. Motivates reps to invest in their territory across years.	No
3. Has uncapped commissions.	No
4. Retains your great reps.	Yes
5. Pays more per dollar sold to those who sell more.	No
6. Treats each dollar of revenue as a dollar of revenue.	No
7. Ensures current customers are treated better than new ones.	Yes
8. Controls the cost of selling.	Yes
9. Aligns rep and management motivations.	No
10. Gives your reps and managers incremental reasons to hustle.	No
Results: 3 of 10	

Health Services Plan retained reps because they reliably paid $200,000 per year to their reps. It treated current customers better since they were not going after new customers. The cost of selling was fixed at five reps times $200,000 per year. It was the lowest cost of selling I had ever encountered (0.25%). It totally suppressed growth.

CHAPTER 17

How to Control the Cost of Selling

"Sales Reps aren't free...they pay you." —*VP Sales to CEO*

I worked recently with a communications startup, and as are all startups, they were perennially low on cash. In an effort to save money and staunch our honestly-unjustifiable burn rate, the CEO suggested we hire only one sales rep and focus on selling through resellers. I appreciated his frugality and agreed with him about the resellers. "But," I argued, "why not hire five reps around the world and have them sell to resellers? Sure it'll cost five times more, but they'll be selling more, so the net cost of sales will be less. We'll have more revenue and actually use less cash." I could tell he wasn't convinced, so I added a touch of drama. "Besides, if they don't sell anything, we probably don't have a viable company anyway."

So how much should you spend?

Set a Minimum Amount, Not a Maximum

You have to decide what you're willing to pay for sales as a percent of revenue or margin and, once set, spend it just as you do for engineering, finance, and operations. Why companies try to continually decrease both the percent and actual cost of selling perplexes me. Selling expenses should be the last to be cut, not the first.

Theoretically, you should spend until the marginal cost of getting the next order equals the incremental margin on the order. This is best illustrated with a Google adwords advertising example. For those unfamiliar with Google adwords, you can continue to bid a higher price per click and get more impressions and, thus, more clicks.

If you're selling a $40 iPhone case that has a cost of $10, then economic theory says you ought to be willing to spend up to $30 to get that order. Annuity revenue companies should be willing to pay up to the lifetime value of that new customer. No one really does this except maybe Groupon.

My rule of thumb for a starting point is to set your cost of selling at 30% of gross margin. So if you sell your Magic Elixir for $100 and your margin is $50, you should invest $15 (a 15% cost of revenue, 30% cost of margin). This is a good starting point. It assumes a one-time sale and no follow-on revenue. At my catalog company, we paid up to $60 to get an initial $50 order from a new customer. That customer would generate over $1,000 in revenue per year over the next three years.

Marketing expenses do not count as sales expenses. Sales expenses are tactical, the immediate measures to get a sale. Marketing, on the other hand, is strategic: brand building, a trade show, an ad in a magazine, or one on TV (unless it's an infomercial, which would be sales). I've seen too many anti-sales executives try to claim they're investing in sales by including marketing expenses in their cost of sales calculation.

Marketing's job is to get what you can sell. Sales' job is to sell what you have. Marketing is responsible for sales two years and beyond. Sales is responsible for two weeks and less. The middle time period is up for grabs.

Catalog Companies

Paper, ink, and postage were pricey. Most consumer catalogs spent about 20% to 30% of revenue, or 40% to 60% of margin, to get orders. The numbers were:

Figure 17.1 Catalog Company Financial Model	
P and L	Percent
Revenue	100%
Cost of Goods	50%
Margin	50%
Catalog Costs (40% of Margin)	20%
Other Costs	20%
Profit	10%

This was a highly predictable business once a mailing list was tested. Customers also had a lifetime value that was high, many buying multiple times per year. The cost of selling to recurring customers was low and the cost of a new customer was high, as it is in most businesses. Many customer catalogs ran 25% of revenue selling and only a 5% profit, but the predictability and control made it a good business.

Hardware Companies

I worked for a computer hardware company after college whose cost of selling numbers approximated what I've seen at most such hardware companies since. They were:

Figure 17.2 Hardware Company Financial Model	
P and L	**Percent**
Revenue	100%
Cost of Goods	40%
Margin	60%
Selling Costs (28% of Margin)	17%
Other Costs	23%
Profit	20%

These companies operate very close to the 30% of margin goal for the cost of selling. This particular example is 28.3%.

Hardware companies had to finance their growth and, as a result, usually grew at a lower, more predictable rate. They had inventory and receivables issues that ate a lot of cash especially during growth periods. By hiring sales reps on a scheduled basis, they would have rookies costing them money, while the mature reps were way below the 17% cost of selling.

Software Companies

I love to work with software companies because they have a 100% gross margin and an infinite supply of inventory. They should spend 30% of revenue, which is also 30% of margin, on selling. They can certainly afford to be generous here, especially if their new customers tend to become repeat buyers and annual support contract buyers.

AsiaSoft gets an $8,000 initial order plus 20% per year in maintenance from each of its new customers. During the next two years, those customers purchase an additional $50,000 worth of products. The lifetime value of their customers is probably $250,000. With customers like that and 100% margins, how much should AsiaSoft spend on sales? I wish they'd spend 30%, but they are trapped in the 25% range. They can't hire reps fast enough and when they do, the new reps get an $8,000 sale ten weeks later, thus dropping the cost of selling back down. AsiaSoft can't get to 30% no matter how much they spend; they only grow faster. It's a great problem to have. Their numbers look like this:

Figure 17.3 Software Company Financial Model	
P and L	Percent
Revenue	100%
Cost of Goods	0%
Margin	100%
Selling Costs (25% of Margin)	25%
Other Costs	40%
Profit	35%

Microsoft averaged a 37% pretax profit in the last 5 years. Compare that to General Electric's 11% or Wal-Mart's 5%. There is a reason VCs like software companies. They're profitable and should liberally invest those profits back into more selling power and some more engineering.

Service Companies

There are a lot of variables with service companies, so it's difficult to present archetypal cost of selling numbers. In general the 30% of margin rule applies. And, as with software companies, service companies' margins are often quite good. Buying Group, a service company I advise, exemplifies this.

Buying Group sells a monthly buying service at $2,000 per month. The margin is nearly 100%. Each sale is a five year contract, meaning $120,000 in revenue from a new customer over five years, plus 80% of customers renew after those five years. Second year reps sell about five new customers per month. How much would you spend to get one of these customers? Here are the figures for a second year rep selling five new customers per month, i.e. adding $10,000 new revenue per month. For simplicity I have ignored the revenue from the customers they closed last year.

Figure 17.4 Buying Group Cost of Selling for a Second Year Rep ($1,000)													
Month	1	2	3	4	5	6	7	8	9	10	11	12	Total
Revenue	$10	$20	$30	$40	$50	$60	$70	$80	$90	$100	$110	$120	$780
Sales Rep's Base	$6	$6	$6	$6	$6	$6	$6	$6	$6	$6	$6	$6	$72
Office/Travel	$2	$2	$2	$2	$2	$2	$2	$2	$2	$2	$2	$2	$24
Commission, 10%	$1	$2	$3	$4	$5	$6	$7	$8	$9	$10	$11	$12	$78
Total Cost of Selling	$9	$10	$11	$12	$13	$14	$15	$16	$17	$18	$19	$20	$174
Net to Company	$1	$10	$19	$28	$37	$46	$55	$64	$73	$82	$91	$100	$606
Cost of Selling %	90%	50%	37%	30%	26%	23%	21%	20%	19%	18%	17%	17%	22%

You can see the wonderful effect of annuity revenue: sales accumulate with time, driving the cost of selling lower and lower. Most service companies, even the non-annuity ones, convert a high percentage of their new customers into repeat customers. Patients tend to stick with their dentist, clients with their lawyer, etc. These are not one-time sales. So it's especially valuable for service companies to invest in selling. They can pay a high percent, knowing any new customers will yield healthy dividends over the long term.

Jumping Out of a Ten Story Window

It is the CEO's job to set the cost of selling rate and then ensure it doesn't get reduced. That's the difficult part—sustaining it. Most VPs of Finance hate spending money, hate selling costs, and hate commissions. As a company grows, the power base moves from engineering to sales to finance. When that happens, it takes a great CEO to thwart the potential damage. With Finance at the helm, liberal credit policies wither; bureaucracy expands; and sales commissions and the number of reps get cut, taking the dollar cost of selling down with them. The VP of Finance then looks like a hero. He has cut costs and yet sales haven't dropped.

*As he passes the fifth floor, the VP Finance says,
"See, I told you nothing bad would happen."*

But they will. Remember sales has inertia, so changes in your cost of selling will have a delayed impact. Imagine if a software company eliminated half of their 50 enterprise sales reps. Selling expenses would be cut in half, and initially revenue, if it moved at all, would probably go up. Why up? Well, the sales cycle is four to six months long so the orders those 50 reps already had in process, the growth they were creating, would likely still come in. The VP of Finance would be knighted. Yet six months later, new orders would be cut in half, halving revenue along with them. The company would be in trouble and the VP of Finance would never be blamed. In fact, company wisdom would be, "Thank God we eliminated those sales positions before revenue went down."

In reality, the revenue you earn today is a reflection of the investments you made, or failed to make, in your sales channel three to six months ago. There will always be forces within the company who want to cut your sales expenditures. They will argue, and accurately so, that such cuts do no immediate harm to revenue. But sales has inertia, and any changes you make, for good or ill, will take months to reverberate. For steady growth, you should stick to your targeted cost of selling rate.

Cutting the percent you spend on sales is best example of jumping out a 10 story window. When going by the 5th floor the VP of Finance says, "See I told you nothing bad would happen."

Why Down is Up

Our cost of selling at Instant Supply traditionally ran at about 16% of revenue, 32% of margin. Then one day our Circulation Director, armed with some back-of-the-envelope math, decided that was too high. "98% of the new catalogs we send are a total waste," he argued. "We can easily cut these and lower our selling costs." On the first point he was technically correct. 98% of the catalogs we sent to new prospects did not result in an order.

Of course said another way, 2% of the catalogs did result in a new customer order. And those new customers kept us growing. Nonetheless, our Circulation Director set out to "fix" our cost of selling, and it almost sank the company.

He reduced prospect mailings, which dropped our cost of selling three points to 13%, and not surprisingly, dropped our new customer acquisition rate along with it. No one noticed that at first, since new customers generally only placed small initial orders. But six months later, when those new customers would normally be placing large follow-on orders, we got nothing, zilch, nada. Sales dropped so fast that suddenly, even with our reduced catalog spend, the cost of selling went up to 18%. And the Circulation Director, who had been swaggering about the office when costs were down and sales were surviving on their own inertia, learned a valuable lesson: Lowering your cost of selling will actually raise your percentage cost of selling.

Instant Supply went from 16% down to 13% and in so doing, ultimately spiked to 18%. When you cut your sales expenses the savings are immediate, but the inevitable revenue losses, which can far outweigh those savings, are delayed. With sales reps these delays and revenue impacts are even more pronounced and take a lot longer to remediate.

Why Up is Down

Likewise, the way to reduce your cost of selling percent is often to spend more. After digging ourselves a hole at Instant Supply, we knew we had to start acquiring new customers again. So we dramatically increased our prospect mailings, spending more in real dollars than we had been before the whole kerfuffle began. We had to wait three months for the fix to take effect, which was a truly scary period, but in the end it worked. New customers came in and revenue went up. Our cost of selling peaked in the low 20% when we first started reinvesting, and then settled at 15%, comfortably below the 18% we saw after the Circulation Director's cuts and below our own historical mark of 16%.

When you spend more on sales, the expenses will eventually be offset by proportionally larger increases in revenue. At Instant Supply we usually budgeted a 16% cost of selling. I wish we had tried to spend 25% instead; we probably would have grown faster and more profitably and thus ended up below 16%. We certainly never would have hit 25% except maybe in the short term.

Why Your Highest Paid Rep is Your Least Expensive Rep

This was covered already but it bears repeating. It is important you, as CEO, remember that your most highly compensated rep is your best deal.

Think about it: who costs you more, a rep selling $4,000,000 per year getting paid $220,000 or one selling $1,000,000 and only making $100,000? Did you ever do the calculation? If you did, you wouldn't be constantly cutting your best reps' compensation.

Overhead is fixed, each rep has one phone and one desk. Assume they have a base of $60,000 and a straight 4% commission. The $1,000,000 rep costs you $100,000 ($60,000 base plus $40,000 commission). That's 10% of sales. The $4,000,000 rep costs you $220,000 ($60,000 base plus $160,000 commission). That's 5.5% of sales. He's half price! Give him a bonus, a new car, and beg him to stay.

The reps you pay the most are in fact the cheapest. And the more they sell, the cheaper they get. So despite what Finance or HR say, you definitely don't want to treat them as fodder for cost cutting.

Riding Your Gravy Train

Your sales department is the engine pulling the train. Everything else—engineering, finance, manufacturing, marketing—are boxcars that need to be pulled along. You need an engine big enough to pull the train ever faster.

If you're one of the lucky companies that has a product or service in high demand, in a large and growing market, then spend like a drunken sailor on selling. (If you're not one of those companies, there are probably some other books you should be reading). I recommend a cost of selling that's 30% of your margin. Once you set your target ratio, be vigilante in maintaining it. Overrule Finance and others who will invariably try to cut sales expenses. Remember that any changes, whether to increase or to cut investments, will take months to be fully felt. And know that cutting your sales investments will lower revenue thereby raising the percentage cost of selling, whereas investing more will spur revenue and thus lower the percentage cost of selling.

Investing in sales is the surest way to grow. If you, as a CEO, overspend anywhere, do it on sales first, engineering second, and nowhere else. Keep your train accelerating.

Figure 17.5 Your Sales Force is your company's engine.
All other departments are boxcars.

161

CHAPTER 18

The Hunter/Farmer Model

CEOs love the Hunter/Farmer Model.

For those not familiar with the Hunter/Farmer model, it has two main components the Sales Rep (Hunter) and the customer account rep (Farmer). Hunters pursue and close new customers. Farmers manage existing customers. Hunters do almost no account management, and Farmers do almost no selling. The model is attractive to CEOs because it allows them to pay sales reps only for new business while shunting account management off to lower-paid non-commissioned or low-commissioned associates.

Sounds great, right?

It depends upon implementation. This is where the CEO can earn the big bucks by protecting the Hunter's ongoing commission check. The positive of Hunter/Farmer model is that it does gives the sales rep more selling time, since he does not have to field customer calls or solve on-going customer problems. The negative is the way it is many times implemented. In the most egregious cases, the Hunter no longer gets any commission for repeat orders from the accounts that he closed. It destroys the dream of continued annuity commission build up.

I am not against giving help to customers or sales reps. In fact, anything you can do to get your reps more selling time is usually good as long as it follows the three priorities of not losing an existing customer, selling more to existing customers, and, only then, getting new customers.

Hunter/Farmer Model for Service Companies

Annuity service industries are a great place to use the Hunter/Farmer model.

Life insurance sales reps: Paid big commission for new customers and paid for renewal customers with a small residual. Most contact after the sale is via customer care and claims. These plans incent the rep for new customers and renewals but still pay an ongoing small commission that keeps the annuity buildup of commissions alive over the long term.

ATM Cash: Paid a good commission for new customers and for renewal of existing customers, especially for early renewal, plus a good continuing commission for maintaining customers. Most contact after the sale was via operations. After placing 100s of ATMs, the reps were locked in, and, due to the margin/length of contract motivation, the customers were locked in as well.

Retail Buying Group: Good commission for closing a new customer, the same for renewing customers after five years plus a residual along the way. Closed customers are serviced by a customer support group on a daily basis, but the sales reps get involved if there are issues. The ongoing annuity payments and especially motivational. After one successful year, reps couldn't afford to leave the company.

Hunter/Farmer Model for Product Companies

While Hunter/Farmer approaches are good for service industries that have a continuing long-term relationship with their customers, they don't work as well for product companies where you continue to sell more existing products or new products to an expanding base inside the same company.

Rugged Computer Corp., Minicomputer Corp., and PA Electronics: Each sale is usually to a different department or government program, so it is the same as closing a new customer. It is somewhat easier since you have good references inside your customer's company. Issue arise when a rep sells a big order that spans years. This takes a tremendous amount of selling effort to close and almost as much to keep closed. This is where the Hunter/Farmer can get abused. CEOs take the position, "I've already paid for that sale, why should I pay commission in year two and three?" This attitude killed Minicomputer Corp's growth and destroyed a fabulous sales engine.

EduCorp, selling educational computer systems, seemed more pure and the Hunter/Farmer wasn't a temptation here. Each school district took a lot of effort and there were few opportunities to sell more to the same customer or across years. I suspect they would attempt to cut commissions if a rep sold a big multi-year, multi-school contract. If this happened, the other great EduCorp sales reps would start looking for a sales job that didn't kill the dream.

AsiaSoft sold a $7,000 license initially and about $100,000 over the next three to five years to the same customer. This one looked ripe for Hunter/Farmer abuse. Luckily they never had time to think about it; they were too busy hiring sales reps that drove 30 to 50% growth.

The one area that Hunter/Farmer is used with no on-going commission and may be appropriate is in "Boiler Room" phone bank operations like selling magazine subscriptions, or raising money for the Police Benevolent Society. These are staffed by short-term hires like college students. They don't care or have any investment in the customers, so paying the biggest commission upfront and none after that is probably right. There probably isn't any after-sales-support either so it should be called just "Hunter/ Abandon".

Test Your Hunter/Farmer Plan

The best way to test your Hunter/Farmer model is to view it from the sales rep's standpoint. Does your sales rep's motivation follow these key priorities?

1. Don't lose a current customer

2. Sell more to existing customers

3. Get new customers.

And do your top reps build up an annuity commission over time that locks them into your company?

If you judge your plan from the rep's viewpoint against these four criteria, you will not go wrong and you won't kill the dream.

Hunter/Farmer abuse isn't new. I still recall 30 years ago my friend, the VP of Finance at a computer printer company, said, "Why should I pay my salesmen for an account they sold last year? I can put a non-commissioned account manager on a buying account a lot cheaper."

That company was hot but disappeared in less than five years. I think the loss of their sales force was a major factor.

Retain, Retain, and Lock Up Your Customers

Your current customers are what make your company viable. They're the reason you can afford to pursue new customers at all. Your reps should be motivated above all to keep your existing customers happy, or a competitor's rep will. Remember: retaining existing customers is the most important job of any sales organization. So incent your reps to service them. Work to create long-term relationships with them.

CHAPTER 19

How to Hire Great Reps

The secret of hiring great reps is to have the highest compensated sales force in your industry. To do this and be financially successful, you should pay a low base and a lucrative commission. So everyone inevitably asks me, "How can we attract talent, especially proven talent, with a low base salary?"

It's a fair question. An experienced sales rep, say in his mid-40s, is not going to leave a good sales job for one that only guarantees him $5,000 per month. He has a mortgage payment and his kids' tuition, and the sports package on Comcast. He's established a lifestyle with fixed expenses that far exceed what you're willing to pay him as a base. So how can you get him to join your team? And how can you recruit the upstart college grad who has better salary options elsewhere and isn't even sure she wants to be a sales rep?

First Motivate your Sales Managers to Hire On Time

Most sales managers will make claim that they can't attract qualified reps with a low base. It does make their short term sales hiring harder, so you need to make sure they are well motivated to hire on time and well.

As I discussed in the *Value of On-Time Hiring* chapter, you should include current reps plus non-hired reps when calculating a manager's sales per rep. In other words, if the company authorizes the manager to hire a new rep, you count that rep as if he is on board from the date of hiring authorization. If the manager's commission is partially based on his sales per rep average, he's highly motivated to find someone great on time. The low base will still be an issue, and your managers will continue to complain, but they will hire great reps on time.

Does this impel managers to simply hire anyone who can fog a mirror? Fortunately not. The manager's long-term compensation hinges on the quality of reps he hires and the averages they generate, so he's motivated to find talent. Ideally managers will have two or three prospects ready to take the job even before the authorization to hire is issued.

How to Use Draws to Hire

There are times when the company needs to help the managers hire. In the case of our Comcast-watching 40-something rep, there's nothing a manager can say to get him to accept a $5,000 base. This is where a "draw" can help.

A "draw" is an advance payment of commission before it is actually earned. It's meant to bridge the gap between being hired and producing recurring revenue. An experienced rep can't come work for you for $5,000 base and wait until they start earning big commissions. So you guarantee them $10,000 per month from the outset. You're including a monthly prepayment of $5,000 of unearned commission. Once the reps start selling, their commissions earned will be used to repay these advances. At least that's the idea.

A standard draw program usually continues until the rep earns commissions above the draw. When your rep starts selling, she doesn't get an actual commission check. She gets an accounting entry showing how much less draw she now has to repay. It's not very motivational, which is why I think most reps hired under a standard draw plan leave the company before the draw is ever paid back. As the draw accumulates, motivation wanes.

Draws are an effective way to attract veteran sales reps. They just have to be done right as shown below.

Two Ways to Fix Draws

1. The Declining Draw

Unlike standard draws which linger on indefinitely, a declining draw is designed to be temporary. It has a scheduled taper. Using the same $5,000/$10,000 example, I would have the draw provide the full $5,000 for the first three months, then have it decline by $500 each month thereafter. By the start of the rep's second year, his base would be the same as all the other reps.

Isn't this a worse deal for the prospective rep? Well, the short answer is yes. You are offering less guaranteed money, and that offer may, therefore, be less attractive. But so be it. Your commissions, for those reps who actually plan to sell, are more generous. And the draw isn't meant to be long-term compensation anyway. It's a temporary bridge to reduce the risk of joining your company and help the rep transition. Once he gains traction and moves up the S-Curve, his commission checks can easily cover his personal spending patterns. I would tell the prospective rep that he will have the $10,000 he's accustomed to for the first few months, and after that, if he sells, he'll be making $20,000.

2. The 50/50 Draw

With a standard draw, if the rep owes $20,000 in draw payments and earns a $5,000 commission the following month, he gets paid nothing. Instead his draw is reduced to $15,000. The entire commission is credited to his draw. It's not very motivating to work for a sale and have nothing to show for it. This is a major downside of paying commissions in advance.

With a 50/50 draw plan, only half the rep's commission is applied toward paying back the draw. This approach gives the rep extra money from the sale and enables the company to recognize his achievement.

Why You Should Pay Commissions Only on Payment of Invoice

I recommend only paying commissions on payment of invoice. Depending upon the type of industry, this is weeks or months after the rep "closed" the sale. This serves as a strong retention motivator for your great reps. If they leave your company, they don't get commission on the sales they have made but not yet been paid for. It's hard to resign if you are leaving $50,000 in unpaid commissions on the table.

For legal reasons, your comp plan/employee contract has to clearly state that the sales rep's job requires more than just getting a purchase order. It requires completing the sale, ensuring the product is delivered and functioning, and most importantly, collecting the receivable. The contract needs to be very specific. There is no commission payment until after collection, and you must be an employee at the time of payment to receive commission.

I once violated this rule. Somehow, I let my VP of Sales talk me into paying 50% of the commission at the time of booking the order and 50% upon getting the invoice paid. Immediately, one of our marginal reps, whose name I have intentionally forgotten, had a friend who worked in purchasing for a large retailer. He persuaded this friend to place a huge order, then earned half of his commission, and promptly quit. We owed him half the commission on that order. But a few weeks later, after we had invested $100,000 building these extra products, the customer called and cancelled the order. That's when we realized we had been duped. We owed the commission, and were stuck with a ton of unsold products.

Attracting Rookies

Attracting rookie reps is different from attracting veteran reps, and you ought to think of these as two separate programs. While I do suggest offering the same base. It will look better to a rookie who wants to get into sales. Rookies' expenses are low since they are usually single and within one to three years out of college.

I still would bolster their base with a supplemental commission program, what I call "recognition accelerators". Instead of guaranteed draw payments, I add incentives above the comp plan that pay for early successes, like: a $500 bonus for the rep's first order, another $500 for the rep's fifth order, $1,000 for the rep's tenth new order and so on. I will set a time limit on these bonuses, for example: the first order bonus expires in two months, the fifth order bonus in four months, and the tenth customer bonus in six months. You can adjust the time frames and dollar amounts based on your industry and the size of the orders involved.

The recognition accelerators usually aren't certain enough to persuade veteran reps. But they attract rookie hires because they see that they can earn more in the near term, and because they like the idea of working for a company that rewards achievement and makes selling fun. And from the company's perspective, the program is well worth its modest price. It helps you attract new reps in spite of a low base, and it helps contain the cost of selling because you're only spending on those who actually sell.

In addition to being an attractant before the rep is hired, the recognition accelerators are also an excellent motivator after he joins. Each accelerator is an opportunity for recognized achievement. When a rookie closes his first order, bells ring and toasts are made. He and his sales manager, who gets a similar but smaller bonus, play hero for the day. And the rep goes to work on hitting the next milestone. I love these accelerators.

Selling the Position

There are numerous methods that will help you hire sales reps:

• Show the prospect what he can earn in years two and three, how he can double his salary every year as he builds his client base because sales is an annuity business.

• Introduce him to the rep that just earned a $250,000 commission check (or won a car). Give the car winner (or top rep) priority parking in the company lot.

• Discuss upward mobility, how fast a sales rep can become a sales manager and earn compounding commissions from the five reps under him.

• Convince him of the quality of your product and its market.

• Show him the hot leads and explain why the job is better than traditional cold calling.

• Describe your company's sales-centric philosophy, how everyone supports the reps. Remind the prospect there will be people around him to help him sell.

• Assure him that, unlike other companies, you always pay commissions and never renegotiate or fiddle with compensation after the fact.

Lord of the Nomads

I had the displeasure of knowing a few highly untalented sales reps back when I was selling minicomputers. We called them the Nomads. I'm sure they still exist today. They were terrible at selling products or services, but very good at selling themselves. They would get together quarterly and discuss various companies' commission plans. At least one of them would always be out of work, having just been fired. But they knew which companies were paying high draws and for how long. So without fail, they would slither onto that company's payroll and collect the draw until they got fired again.

That's the kind of "talent" you don't want to attract. The declining draw or performance draw are good Nomad repellents. You want to attract reps by offering to reward their performance, not their pulse. The best way to detect Nomads is that they constantly quiz you about the draw and its duration. They want to get paid whether they sell or not.

CHAPTER 20

The Power of Aligning Motivations

"Our sales reps ought to do it for the good of the company or I'll fire the whole lot of them."
--Angry CEO

"Why aren't the reps signing more long-term contracts?"

"How come the reps aren't converting customers' equipment instead of selling expensive new machines we have to pay for?"

"Why aren't the phone reps referring the big deals to the enterprise sales force?"

"Why don't we get more new customers?"

Answers to these questions are almost always found in your sales compensation plan. Reps will do what your comp plan motivates them to do, not what you want them to do, and not what your managers badger them to do. Likewise, sales managers and the VP of Sales, or anyone who's paid on commission, will be influenced by the nature of that commission. So write your plan to align everyone's motivations with your goals. And as new goals develop, revise the plan to maintain that alignment. If there's a problem, read the plan from the reps' or managers' point of view and see what you would do if you were them. Then fix it.

Align Reps with Management

We previously saw how ATM Cash inadvertently let their customers slip to month-to-month contracts. Management certainly wanted long-term contracts, where the customers weren't vulnerable to competitors, and revenue was predictable over the long term. But the reps didn't get paid more to sign them, and they were harder to sell. It was purely a motivation problem. We fixed it by changing the comp plan to pay a higher rate of commission for longer contracts especially those with higher margins. We motivated the reps to do what management wanted. Alas, this wasn't ATM Cash's only motivation problem.

For ATM Cash, the more cash dispensing machines they operated, the more cash they dispensed and the more fees they collected. Each machine was like a sales rep. Many customers had existing "Bill Breaking" machines that could be converted to ATM functionality. This was ideal; the company made transaction fees and didn't incur the $8,000 to $12,000 cost of a new ATM. It was the most profitable transaction ATM Cash could do. Unfortunately, and much to the CEO's chagrin, their sales reps continued to sell new machines, not convert existing Bill Breakers.

When I pointed out the obvious, that the company didn't pay any commission on Bill Breaker conversions but paid handsomely for new machine placement, the CEO went a bit apoplectic. "Those damn reps," he roared. "They ought to do it for the good of the company. They should be team players; hell, we're feeding their family."

"Good points," I said. "But wouldn't it be better to line up their motivation with the company's?"

It was a simple matter to fix, and it worked spectacularly well. We started paying commission on Bill Breaker conversions and reduced the commission on new machine placements. The CEO stopped screaming at his best reps and started screaming at his comp plan author. (He was the author.)

I have a friend who sells for a heavy equipment dealer: tractors, fork lifts, things of that nature. His company harangues their reps for not getting leases renewed early. But when a rep actually does it, he loses commission dollars. Under their comp plan, a renewal lease pays lower commission than a new customer contract. So when a rep renews a lease after, say, three years of a five year contract, the company rescinds the high commission for the remaining two years of the original contract and starts paying the lower renewal commission rate. This makes the commission negative. The rep has to pay the company for having done what they wanted him to do. Now, are you angry at the rep for not renewing early? Or are you angry at yourself for approving the comp plan?

Align Reps with Reps

Believe it or not, it can be good to foster cooperation, not competition, amongst your reps. AsiaSoft had an internal phone sales group to handle smaller orders and an external enterprise sales group to handle larger, more complex orders. Many times the phone sales reps would stumble on a potentially big account. The policy was that the phone rep was supposed to refer any customer with the potential of spending over $30,000 to the enterprise reps. But, if the phone rep closed the $30,000+ order himself, we paid him the commission. You can probably guess how many referrals the enterprise reps received: none.

Remember AsiaSoft was selling software. Software has a 100% margin and an infinite supply of instantly deliverable product, plus a potentially high rate of product obsolesce. So you need to move product fast and can afford a liberal cost of selling to do it. For AsiaSoft the fix was simple: we paid double commission. If a phone rep referred a lead to an enterprise rep who then closed an order in the next 12 months, both reps got paid. The phone rep received 10% commission and the enterprise rep 6%, for a total of 16% cost to the company.

Now the phone reps happily referred leads, and our big orders increased, because we have experienced reps focused on these larger accounts.

The only unanticipated side effect came when a puckish phone rep figured out that if he referred all his leads to the enterprise reps, he had his own sales force personally selling for him. We promoted him to an enterprise rep, even though strictly speaking, he was not following the rules. We wanted that level of creativity on the enterprise team. Besides, it wasn't his fault we had a flaw in the comp plan. It was ours.

Why You Should Beat Up the Comp Plan Author, Not Your Sales Reps

The sales rep does whatever your comp plan drives him to do. You are telling him, perhaps without even noticing it, that you want him to pursue certain situations and avoid others. Your yells and screams won't change his daily actions; only a change in the comp plan will. The same is fundamentally true of your sales managers, VPs, even departments—they must be incented to do what you want them to do.

- If your reps consistently sell products that are less profitable, it is because that's what you're paying them to do.

- If the sales manager is trying to delay a delivery to the next fiscal year while the rep is desperately trying to ship it this year, it is because that's what their conflicting plans tell them to do.

- If I spend three months convincing my boss that my territory is dry instead of selling, it is because that's what my comp plan tells me to do.

- If your reps pocket high-value leads, or your website stops referring people to your retail store, it is because that's what you ordered them to do.

- If ever your reps are not doing what you want them to do, take a look at your comp plan to figure out why.

CHAPTER 21

The Illusion of Compensation Plan Savings

I flew to China a couple years ago for AsiaSoft's quarterly Board meeting. We met at the company's R&D facility outside Shenzhen, in an American-style R&D building that boasts 350 full-time engineers, all employees of AsiaSoft. The meeting started out well: sales had exceeded projections; two new products were ahead of schedule; and they were hiring sales reps as fast as they could. Wall Street bankers were salivating.

Then the AsiaSoft executives began to explain the "problem" they had with a 24 year old phone sales rep. The rep, with a $3,000 per month base salary, had just helped land a $3.1 million software sale. "But she isn't even an enterprise sales rep," they said. "She's just a phone rep. Now, according to our compensation plan, we're supposed to pay her $310,000?" I shifted nervously in my seat, sensing what was coming next. "Obviously that's not going to happen. We'll negotiate her down to $100,000. That's enough."

I bit my tongue, fearing the tirade I was about to unleash. I had visions of having to find my own way to the airport and waiting for a standby flight home after they tossed me off the Board. My friend and fellow board member Jen Smith was less restrained:

"Have you not heard a bloody thing Bill has been saying? This rep is your new hero, your poster sales rep. Her story will inspire all your other reps to sell more. Not only pay her in full, pay her with one of those giant four-foot long checks like Publishers Clearing House and award it to her in front of the entire company."

I don't know if AsiaSoft's executives got Jen's Ed McMahon Publisher's Clearing House reference, but they accepted her argument. The sales rep got her $310,000, and her giant novelty check.

After that commission check presentation, the other phone sales reps came in early, worked late, and almost doubled their number of calls and demos. They were selling with hope of their big payday, and they were doing so with confidence they would get paid when they landed the big one. Hiring more reps became easy. "See Irene? She made $310,000 on one sale last year." Suddenly the $3,000 per month base we were paying wasn't a hiring impediment.

The real credit belongs to AsiaSoft's executives who, against their initial instincts, paid the commission in full. They could have negotiated down to $100,000. Instead, AsiaSoft recognized that when you pay a big commission, you're inspiring all your sales reps, current and future, to bring in more revenue. And conversely, if you renege, you lose far more in future revenue than you save in current payouts.

Remember the company got paid, the investors got paid, the VP Finance and CEO got paid. Why shouldn't your rep get paid?

The Minicomputer Corp. Compensation Plan Disaster!

I have never seen a sales comp plan change for the better from the reps' perspective. Think about that statement for a minute: **Any revision to a sales comp plan is almost certainly negative to your sales reps, especially your best ones.** Each change makes their sales life worse until they're finally compelled to leave.

The most egregious example of a change in comp plans happened while I was a rep for Minicomputer Corp. It destroyed the company.

As Minicomputer Corp. grew, management necessarily delegated various responsibilities lower and lower in the organization. Regretfully, this included the sales comp plan, one of the major keys of their success to date. And they delegated it to the Human Resources Department, which is maybe half a step better than the Finance Department.

HR set out, of course, to cut selling costs, probably in order to hire more HR managers. What HR came up with was a plan that killed the dream. If an account averaged over $300,000 per year for the previous three years, then half the commission for that account was eliminated the following year. In other words, if I sold $1 million to Aero Corp. in year one, and again in year two, I only got commission on $500K in year two, since half was eliminated. I wouldn't earn a penny on the first $500K I sold in year two. Minicomputer Corp. reasoned that the customer had developed their software and couldn't change computer vendors. The sales rep had already been paid for the sale and now orders would just roll in. In HR's mind there was no reason to pay the rep full commission in following years.

The new plan offered me an 88% pay cut for selling more than I had the year prior. My boss asked, "What about Bill? He earned $252,000 in commission last year, and under your plan this year, he will get only $60,000, even if he sells more than last year?"

To which the VP of HR, with his characteristic charm, replied, "Screw him. I only make $58,000."

Look at What This Comp Change Did

1. It devalued the best sales reps, the ones that sold big multiyear contracts.

2. It punished the best customers. I was not motivated to service an account that was 50% pro bono.

3. It demotivated big multi-year sales.

The sales reps figured out instantly to keep all customers below $300,000 per year, if you wanted to get paid.

Needless to say, the sales force was shocked. Minicomputer Corp. had the best sales reps in the industry, lowest base, and highest average compensation. In only six months, 90+% of the best reps resigned. Their dream had been taken away.

Yet while our résumés were being updated, Minicomputer Corp. was celebrating increased profits, due to reduced commission payments. Profits went even higher when we all resigned. They didn't have to pay the base salaries, and the orders, that we had sold, kept coming in as HR predicted. For a time, that is.

The irony is when you cut sales compensation, profits go up because selling has inertia. When you improve a plan, it takes time to drive sales up. When you destroy a plan, it takes time for the orders to stop coming. But they did stop for Minicomputer Corp.

Sales cratered within two years. Big accounts switched to the former reps' new employers. Growth stopped, and profits were non-existent. Minicomputer Corp. became an also ran after years of 50 to 100% sales growth. It was sad.

I left four months after the comp plan change, when my commissions from the previous year's sales had played out. I had four great years there, with one "Rookie of the Year" award and three "Salesman of the Year" awards, only to be forced out by a faceless VP of HR. I moved on though, starting a company that sold accessories to Minicomputer Corp.'s customers. I think, though I'm not sure, that it became a bigger company than Minicomputer Corp. at one point in time. I have to thank HR for that.

Minicomputer Corp. tried to wring savings from the worst possible place: their best sales reps. The CEO erred in delegating the comp plan to human resources, but really blew it when he accepted the changes they proposed. HR believed, as most non-sales employees believe, that sales reps were overpaid, and in the interest of cutting those costs, they cratered the entire company.

It can be very tempting to cut sales comp or try to withhold commission due. It's low hanging fruit for a budget hawk, especially one who doesn't value sales reps. And the immediate effect of such cuts is often positive. But if you reduce the sales compensation line in your budget, then you need to also reduce the revenue line six month later, because that is exactly what you are really cutting. Every dollar "saved" on comp is an exponential loss in revenue, albeit a deferred one. "Savings" are an expensive illusion.

Sales comp is an investment in revenue production. As CEO, you shouldn't allow any changes to the comp plan without due consideration involving discussion with your top reps, and an analysis of what you would do if you were a sales rep when the change was implemented.

SECTION 4

HOW TO MANAGE

CHAPTER 22

The Psychology of Sales

The Worn Shoes of a Sales Rep

Selling is a brutal way to make a living. Other than being CEO, I believe selling is the hardest job in any company, bar none. That's why it pays so much. Not many people want to do it; most would hate doing it; and only a few can do it. Not many of them can do it for long. Go see the play or movie *Glengarry Glen Ross* or *Death of a Salesman.*

• Selling is lonely. Most of the time you face the customer by yourself. And you're out there trying to overcome handicaps imposed by your own company, rarely blessed with a product your customer wants more than your competitor's. I remember David Packard, the cofounder of HP, telling his new hire sales class, "If I had the best products at the lowest price with instant delivery, I wouldn't need you guys."

• Selling is rejection. If your company has a 20% market share that means on average you get rejected four out of five times. And that's not even counting all the times you get rejected by people who aren't in the market at all. Yet we expect sales reps to knock on doors with enthusiasm every day. That's very tough.

• Sales reps are disrespected. Joe Isuzu said it all. While he was describing his car, the caption read, "He's lying." Conventional wisdom says, "Sales reps cheat, drink too much, don't tell the truth, and don't work very hard." In my opinion sales reps are among the hardest working and most honest people I know.

• Sales reps are viewed by corporate as a problem.

"Why can't she sell what we have?"
"Why does he need a bigger discount?"
"Why can't she control her customer?"
"He said he would get the order this week. Where the hell is it?"

• Sales reps are undervalued.

"Why should I pay him commission when he didn't sell it?"
"Why should she make $120,000 a year for just taking orders?"
"I have more education and work longer hours, so why does he get all the money?"

• And then there's the cold calling.

Imagine what it's like to call 50 people you've never met, knowing 49 of them will openly resent you for doing it. Now try to stay upbeat and motivated as each one unleashes a more dismissive rejection than the last, except perhaps the 50th, who will listen earnestly and then decide against buying. Cold calling is an amalgam of all the worst things about sales: the loneliness, the rejection, the disrespect. It is one of the reasons sales reps get paid a lot, and the main reason most people are unwilling to go into sales.

It's a hard knock life for us.

Dirty Jobs

Selling is a dirty job. One company I consulted for had three offices, each with three sales teams. Each sales rep made 60 cold calls per day, looking to sell a specialized internet service to small businesses. The reps would average five sales per month. Five "Yeses" to 1,320 "Nos" (60 calls 22 working days). Brutal, but these reps loved the challenge, loved the recognition, and loved the camaraderie. Their managers rang a bell for each sale. The sales rep standings were posted on a computer screen in front of them. They had sales contests each month. And the beer would flow at five o'clock (yes, they actually had a kegerator in the office).

Another consulting client had Stanford and Harvard MBAs cold calling 150 CEOs each month hoping to get private company information and, if it met their private equity firm's criteria, schedule a meeting with the CEO. Essentially, they were trying to invest in successful companies that didn't need the investment specifically because they were successful. The sales team, staffed by some of the brightest and most educated young people in America, hit the phones day after day. The reps averaged one deal every two years. That's over 3,000 calls to get one "Yes". Grueling perhaps, but those young guns loved their job and killed for the recognition they got, from managers and peers alike, when they closed a deal.

I can empathize. When I was selling for Minicomputer Corp., we received thousands of "leads" from the advertising department every month. They came from computer magazine ads where the reader could circle a postcard to get more information. Most of our reps ignored them; conventional wisdom was these folks were all "Literature Collectors". Why anyone wanted to collect computer sales literature escaped me. Why thousands of people per month wanted to collect computer sales literature really escaped me. And since I was recently married, had a new baby on the way and no sales prospects, I diligently called about ten of these leads per day. I made 50 phone calls to get one appointment. When I actually met with a potential customer, only one in three would be qualified. That's 150 calls to get one decent prospect, a lot of frustrating and hard work, but ultimately lucrative work.

Think of the dirty job your sales reps endure day after day, the perseverance and confidence it takes to find that elusive "Yes" amidst a deluge of "Nos". Sale reps learn to protect themselves psychologically, to deflect the rejection and keep going. Their good spirit and camaraderie can help turn an otherwise horrible job into a great one. But they must have your support and recognition. Without that, selling is a very dirty job.

The Fun Just Doesn't Stop

Selling is psychologically the hardest job in any company. Reps are a strange combination of ego and fragility. They hear "No" more than a three year old at Toys "R" Us, and they hear it every working day. They work long hours (yes, dinners and drinking count as work). Then, when they expect support for what they consider a reasonable request, they hear corporate yell, "Hell no."

It's very hard to keep motivated selling. Each month you start with a big goose egg behind your name in the sales journal. Competing sales reps all appear to have better products, better delivery, lower prices, better service and better quality. And when you do land an order you hear, "He didn't really sell it; the CEO or VP of Engineering did." It's a tough road. A compassionate Sales Manager and supportive CEO can keep you going.

Sympathize with your reps, elevate their status within the company, and support them. Ask your VP of Sales, your VP of Finance, your VP of Operations, and anyone else in the company: "What are you doing to help the reps sell more?"

CHAPTER 23

Why Good Sales Reps Need Great Sales Managers

"Go to a bar. Go to the library. Go play golf. But get your butt out of this office. If you haven't noticed, there are no customers here."
— My best sales manager

I am not a good sales manager, but I had the pleasure of working for two great sales managers, having two work for me, and the honor to watch another dozen at VC funded companies. I am mostly in awe of their motivational skills, and they think they have the easiest job in the world. For them, it may be; they think they do nothing. Here's my view of what great sales managers do, wittingly or not:

1. They keep the fragile ego of sales reps intact.

2. They keep the stupid corporate rules at bay.

3. They come up with reasons to make one more sales call.

4. They focus on closing.

5. They get their reps the resources they need.

6. They use excuse deprivation.

1. Keep the Fragile Ego of Sales Reps Intact

Selling is a tough, at times demoralizing, job. Even the most confident sales rep gets discouraged.

I had the incredible luck of working for a brilliant sales manager in my first selling job at Minicomputer Corp. I was selling minicomputers, or I was supposed to be selling them anyway. The territory I was hired to cover had bought zero computers the year before. I was a complete rookie in a seemingly arid territory, later renamed "A Fat Patch" once I sold a ton. So what does the world's greatest sales manager do? He built my confidence.

"Keep pushing. Remember, we can't do any worse than last year," he would tell me.

"Here is a lead, call him."

"There has to be a lot of business at Stanford; they get a lot of grants. Try taking their head of purchasing to lunch." He kept encouraging me, pushing me to make one more sales call.

As I showed fledgling signs of viability, he would praise often.

"Bill, tell all of us about the demo that landed Aero Corp."

"Good job on Stanford Radio Astronomy, man, DEC will hate losing that one."

A year later, when I was finally selling in decent numbers, he showed me how he motivated his established reps. I had been in the office for three days straight trying to reconcile my commission statement. He walked up and said: "Bill, what are you doing in the office three days in a row? You are driving me nuts. I know there are no customers around here, so I know you're not selling anything and I can't stand it. Go to a bar. Go to the library. Go play golf. But get your butt out of this office or I'm going to go crazy." He wasn't berating me or undermining my confidence. He was reminding me, in a humorous yet powerful way, to focus on making sales calls.

As I progressed as a new sales rep at Minicomputer Corp., his treatment of me evolved from nurturing to impelling. Yet he was always positive, always praising. He, like all great sales managers, knew how to keep his reps motivated and, most importantly, to keep them confident.

2. Keep the Stupid Corporate Rules at Bay

The time your reps spend on bookkeeping and complying with inane rules, is time they are not selling. That's money out of your company's pocket. How much are those rules worth to you?

My Minicomputer Corp. sales manager had some classic ways of bending the rules for his sales reps. One day he told us: "Okay guys, someone in accounting noticed that you all drive either 15 or 20 miles to each account. Either randomize it or let me do it for you. I don't want you wasting time recording mileage." He enjoyed gaming our "bureaucratic filings", what the company called "factory requests". He would tell us: "I need your sales forecasts. You know the drill. Forecast high or you'll have long delivery times. We need to get manufacturing to order a lot of parts so if you do happen to sell anything, something'll be there to ship."

3. Come up with Reasons to Make One More Sales Call

Sales reps often need an extra push to pursue a lead or close a deal. A great sales manager offers creative reasons and new opportunities for reps to try once more.

"I saw Norm at a cocktail party. Have you been out there? It sounds like he's toying with a new project."

"The CEO is coming to town. Why don't you take him to meet Pat at Edusoft and then use him to get you into Drug Corp. where you haven't busted through the front door yet?"

"Have you considered calling on BioRad? Their supplier is having delivery problems, and they have to be frustrated. This could be our chance to steal the deal."

These creative nudges from the sales manager will result in more activity and more revenue.

4. Focus on Closing

My boss at Minicomputer Corp. had one suggestion I still remember, and occasionally use, 30 years later. He said, "Before you do anything else each morning, do something that gets each of your top five prospects closer to closing. Get their quote out. Take them to lunch with a satisfied customer. Get them back to the factory, anything that helps them make a positive decision."

I started doing this first thing each morning, and soon I needed new leads because all my hot prospects had closed. My manager made me a great closer with this one simple suggestion.

I should point out that he also told me the difference between being a resource for your customer and being a pest: if you call with useful new information that helps your customer make a positive decision, you are a resource; if you call to "touch base" or "check in", you are a pest. Really great advice.

5. Give Your Reps the Resources They Need

The sales manager should ensure that sales reps have whatever they need to sell as much as possible.

One day Joe Williams, my regional manager at Minicomputer Corp., said to me, "I'm heading for the corporate offices tomorrow. Is there anything I can do to help you?" Cheerfully, I gave him a list of about 72 action items I needed for my customers. Not only did Joe get them done, he revised our processes to obviate many of the items for good. He also succeeded in getting me a personal assistant at the factory to solve problems in the future. In one swoop, Greg doubled my selling time. That is great sales management.

6. Use Excuse Deprivation

Sales reps, like anyone else I suppose, occasionally proffer excuses for why they can't land a certain order. The sales manager should solicit these reasons and then help the rep overcome them. I call this process "excuse deprivation". It works well.

Essentially, you take away any excuse that keeps the customer from buying. Well, most excuses, you can't take away the fact they have to pay for the product. As a result of this advice, my catalog company had the following business offer:

Shipped the same day

30 days to pay

45 day no-hassle returns policy

Lifetime guarantee on most products

Why wouldn't you purchase? No excuses.

Most on-line companies do all this now, but direct selling organizations have yet to treat their customers this well.

What Would You Want as a Sales Manager?

When you consider what makes a great sales manager, try thinking of yourself as a sales rep, either an inexperienced kid in a barren territory or a self-assured veteran sales rep making more than the CEO. What would you want in a manager? What would help make you sell more? I believe it's someone who recognizes your successes, one who supports you in your struggles, someone on your side, and someone who makes timely and useful suggestions. The great managers I've worked for, and who have worked for me, all shared these key traits.

CHAPTER 24

Sales Motivators

"Give me enough metals and ribbons and I will conquer the world."
—Napoleon Bonaparte

When I set up my catalog company in the UK, I instituted an "Employee of the Year" award. It was just a plaque. I probably should have attached a $500 check to it, but I didn't. It was just a $30 plaque and a handshake, but tons of recognized achievement.

When I presented the award to our warehouse supervisor, Mick, at the annual employee banquet, he started to cry in front of the whole company. "This is the happiest day of my life," he said. It was an inspiring scene. His wife, in typical British wit, lightened the mood, "No it isn't Mick. That was when you married me."

At Minicomputer Corp I won the "Rookie of the Year" award followed by three "Salesman of the Year" awards. That was over 30 years ago. I still have the plaques hanging in my office. I still smile when I glance at them and I still remember the look of pride on my wife's face when my name was announced.

The Incredible Power of Recognized Achievement

Most CEOs think the major motivator for sales reps is their commission check. It's not. It is recognized achievement. Reps, and all your other employees, crave recognition for performance they are proud of. If you want to maximize revenue per rep, you should shower your reps with awards and recognition. It costs you little and it keeps them highly motivated. It also reminds you and your managers how important the reps truly are. Napoleon was right: recognition is the great motivator.

As my friend who works in equipment sales said, "Things like recognition meetings where your name is being called when you hit your number or do really well are a great motivator." She paused. "I may be a rarity in my line of work, but I really am as much about the appreciation and 'rah-rah' pats on the back as I am about the financial incentives." She is wrong, she's not a rarity.

It's fun motivating your reps. Here are eight specific tactics I have used successfully and recommend:

1. Awards

The $3.00 Matchbox Car

Aside from the tearful Mick and my own treasured Minicomputer awards, the $3.00 Matchbox Car is probably my favorite award and favorite award story. This one also came about at Minicomputer Corp. My boss, the best sales manager in the world, needed a way to recognize his reps' achievement, but the Company was incredibly cheap and he had no "award budget". So he went out and bought $3.00 matchbox cars.

Whenever anyone closed a new account, he would glue a matchbox car to an index card with the customer name, date and revenue typed on it. These trophies, which looked suspiciously like a second grader's diorama, would be presented at the monthly sales meeting as a "Hot Shoe" award. (In parlance from the days of door-to-door selling, a "Hot Shoe" was a good sales rep.) We treasured those stupid cars. I closed 19 new accounts that year; people jokingly referred to the top of my bookcase as the "Parking Lot". I loved it. Would I have closed those accounts anyway? Honestly, probably not. The recognition, embodied in some slapdash trinket, drove us.

Thirty years later, when I advised a major private equity firm on improving their sales program, I told them the matchbox car story and suggested they publicly recognize any associate who successfully closed a deal. This is a multi-billion dollar firm with money to burn. I expected they would give an engraved piece of Steuben glassware or a gold bar with the associate's name on it. Three years later, when I asked a partner if they had instituted any of my suggested programs, he said, "Of course we did, the best of which is the Matchbox Car Award." I was stunned and a little amused by their pedantry…or stinginess. They had taken

Aero Corp.
5/27/2012
$10 Million

Figure 24.1 the $3 Matchbox Car Award

me literally, and to this day they are giving out $3.00 matchbox cars as a reward for multimillion dollar private equity deals. It proves beyond a shadow of doubt that recognition is the key, not the actual award. Just give something, and do it publicly and put the recipient's name on it.

2. Reports

How to Count a Sale Three Times

One of the best ways to motivate sales reps is to tap into their incredible competitive spirit by publishing monthly sales per rep reports. This recognizes achievement at the top and motivates the bottom to get moving upward. In order for new reps to end up on top and get the encouragement they often sorely need, sort the report by monthly percentage of quota. (Stop, before you go off and try to pay commission based on percentage of quota, re-read the "Basics of Great Comp" chapter. Quota is only an agreement between the sales manager and the rep as to what the territory should produce in the coming year. It has nothing to do with compensation.)

I love this sales report. It ranks sales reps by percentage of monthly bookings quota, and shows shipments both monthly and year to date.

		Figure 24.1 Palo Alto Office Sales Report								
May Sales Report		**Bookings**							**Shipments**	
Palo Alto Branch		**May**			**YTD**				**May**	**YTD**
Rank	**Sales Rep**	**Actual**	**Quota**	**%**	**Actual**	**Quota**	**%**		**Actual**	**Actual**
1	Joe Peters	$ 84,000	$ 25,000	336%	$ 94,000	$ 125,000	75%		$ 20,000	$ 44,00
2	Mary Jones	$ 120,000	$ 100,000	120%	$ 600,000	$ 500,000	120%		$ 240,000	$ 450,00
3	Bill Marold	$ 80,000	$ 75,000	107%	$ 150,000	$ 375,000	40%		$ 67,000	$ 90,00
4	Susan Wright	$ 20,000	$ 25,000	80%	$ 38,000	$ 125,000	30%		$ 10,000	$ 15,00
5	Mary Hill	$ 150,000	$ 200,000	75%	$ 1,300,000	$ 1,000,000	130%		$ 270,000	$ 850,00
6	Ronnie Carter	$ 30,000	$ 50,000	60%	$ 150,000	$ 250,000	60%		$ 27,000	$ 95,00
7	Brian Gilly	$ 12,000	$ 40,000	30%	$ 240,000	$ 200,000	120%		$ 90,000	$ 180,00

This Report Motivates Multiple Ways:

1. As a rep, you get recognized three times per sale. First you show up on the booking column; then the sale shows up in the shipped column; and finally, upon payment of the invoice, you get the actual commission check.

2. It recognizes reps, even ones well below YTD quota, for a good month. It's like match play in golf: you may not be doing well on the overall score, but you can still par a hole (or a month) now and then.

3. It holds the best performing rep up as an example by the YTD booking and shipping column.

4. It enables anyone to calculate how much the highest performing rep is making in commission.

If you don't publish your monthly sales by rep, you are missing a simple, powerful motivator.

3. Contests

Monthly, or at least quarterly, sales contest are a must. The key to running great contests is weekly reporting, similar to the monthly sales report above. Remember: recognition, not the actual reward, is the purpose of the contest. So frequent, public exposure is paramount, whether it's a chart on the wall with toy airplanes racing toward Hawaii or a thermometer showing the sales heat.

Sales contests should have a specific goal. At Minicomputer Corp I remember three: a Fortune 500 contest, a new product contest, and a new customer contest. The format was largely the same for all three. There was a minor reward of $50 for each point (earned via a F500 sale, new product sale, or new customer sale) and big prizes for the overall 1st, 2nd and 3rd place finishers. For example, 1st place got a trip to Hawaii, 2nd a big screen TV, and 3rd a $500 gift certificate.

Each Friday the managers published the report with our standings. It spurred our friendly rivalries and forced us to plan ahead. I remember even involving my customer in the contest; "I need this order by Friday so I can win a trip to Hawaii." Later they would ask how I was doing. My customers were cheering for me to win. So too was my wife, whose brother lived in Hawaii. We wanted to visit, especially if it was free.

Alas, I came in second. To this day I know the other rep was really good, but more crafty than good. He held POs until the last day so I couldn't get my customers to order more and win. I'm still mad I didn't win, but I do have a nice TV.

Add Your VPs to Your Sales Contests

I've seen this work very well. It was the last quarter of the year and Graphicsoft was way behind their sales plan. The CEO had heard my rants about sales contests and one upped me by involving his VPs. He assigned every VP to a rep (they had five of each), and made both eligible for a trip to Hawaii. This was magic. The VP of Finance learned more about sales and gained more sales empathy than he would have with anything we could have done. His wife wanted the trip and he, by damn, was going to win it. Sure enough, he did. But it wasn't just him supporting his rep.

Goaded by their VPs, the whole company rallied to sales. Any question was answered in seconds. Any special engineering was approved in minutes. And sales skyrocketed. It had a permanent positive effect on the culture of the company. I just couldn't get them to hire more than five sales reps.

4. Accelerators

Accelerators are a motivating tool you should codify in your sales comp plan. They're remarkably effective. At AsiaSoft we had end-of-quarter accelerators. If a rep reached the first plateau of $200,000 in revenue for the quarter, he received a $1,000 bonus. If he hit $300,000, he got a $3,000 bonus. It worked in spades. Every third month sales would go up 50% over the prior two months. The reps would hustle to get above the plateau and earn the recognition and money.

Then AsiaSoft took the accelerators away, at the behest of the VP of Finance who claimed they were too hard to calculate. (Remember what I said about letting Finance change your comp plan?) Not surprisingly, sales in the third month of each quarter remained flattened. I raised a mild fit at a board meeting, and am pleased to report the accelerators are now back in place and end of quarter sales are back to 50% above first and second months.

At Social Media, we implemented a bonus for the fifth and tenth new customers signed each month. In the past, the reps usually only landed three new customers per month. Now most are above five and a few are at ten. The spiff is only $300 for the fifth customer, but it is $300 and recognition.

At Buying Group, an annuity sales company, good reps added 50 new retailers each year, mostly in the last quarter. This drove management nuts. The year would be made, or lost, in the last month. We put into place an end of quarter bonus for booking 10 customers by the end of the first quarter, 20 by the end of the second quarter, or 35 by the end of the third quarter. To the reps, it felt like free money, a bonus for something they were eventually going to do anyway. But for us, it quickly smoothed the bookings across the year. And most reps' overall sales for the year went up as well, since they had more in the bag going into the fourth quarter.

One of the best side effects of sales motivators is they remind you and your managers to pause and recognize your reps.

Accelerators are especially valuable on this front because they set your recognition on a discrete schedule: monthly, quarterly, etc.

5. Camaraderie

The Recognition Club – United's Global Services

If you fly United, you understand their levels and the perks that go with them. It works so well they keep adding another layer: Premier Associate, then Silver, Gold, Platinum, and now Global Services. You should do the same with your sales reps. You should have a 100% Club, President's Club, or Ten Million Dollar Club.

The club should include perks like a resort trip for a three-day weekend. All the VPs and the CEO should attend. I would even pick some key engineers to come interact with your best reps. Spouses should be invited as well so they can express their pride as their spouses get honored.

The idea is to create a social element to your motivation, an elevated status that makes your reps feel part of something cool and privileged, that fosters camaraderie and makes the job fun. My friend Jake in B-to-B sales had no use for pizza parties but speaks highly of his club trips:

> If you get three new accounts in a quarter for two consecutive quarters, you're included on an all-expense-paid overnight trip with food and beverage provided. It's pretty cool to get included, not only because of the recognition, but for the mere fact that it's usually a really fun event. We went to Great America on a party bus

loaded with great Napa wine. Another time we took an Amtrak train on a reserved car to Tahoe. I've resolved to never miss a trip. I hate to say it, but they've actually made me work harder.

Best CEO Question Ever

When I went to my first 100% Club, the CEO said: "You are the most successful sales reps in our company. We know all the stuff we do wrong, you've told us repeatedly all year long. What I want to hear is what we do right that enabled all of you you to sell over a $1 million of our products. Our VPs are here to listen carefully, so shoot."

That was the best meeting I had ever attended. Great ideas flowed. We went away really fired up and corporate had some really great feedback. The reps developed a bond with the company and the VPs.

6. Excitement

The 100% commission plan

I love it when a CEO takes these concepts and improves them, as Fred Cowell did at Internet Ad Sales. Fred's company was in LA, so he hired graduates directly out of USC and UCLA for sales positions. Even back when grads were in demand, he didn't have a problem hiring because the comp plan he wrote paid 100% commission on the first $5,000 in sales each month. 100%! Everyone wants to be paid 100% commission.

After the first $5,000 at 100%, the plan was more normal:

10% for the next $100,000 and 15% for anything after that. Fred effectively made the base salary variable, and the reps loved it. Instead of having a plan with a $5,000 base plus a commission, he disguised the base as a 100% commission. And when he did hire a non-productive rep, which was rare with this plan, he didn't have to pay them. It was brilliant. I don't think even the worst performing rep ever sold below $5,000 per month since that was his own money.

One of his reps, a 22 year old ex-USC cheerleader, made $331,000 her first year selling. The company made about $2,500,000 in additional margin because of her. She worked hard and was effective. She's still selling at another of Fred's companies and still breaking the bank.

Okay, I can hear you say, "Cheerleader?" What you may not realize is that at USC becoming a cheerleader is extremely competitive. Anybody who can win that competition is someone you should hire as a sales rep immediately, along with any star athletes, Olympians and so on. Athletes make great sales reps: they love competition and the recognized achievement of winning.

7. Qualification

Give Reps Very Hot Leads

The CEO of Graphicsoft was extremely frustrated. He was spending hundreds of thousands of dollars on advertising and personally writing a monthly article in Graphics Software Magazine. His efforts were producing 400 to 500 sales leads each month, but his reps were ignoring them.

He wanted to institute a system whereby the sales rep would have to report on each lead and what he had done with it. I reminded him of my sales manager's old quote: "You can get a rep to report whatever you want, but that doesn't mean he's doing it." To get him to do what you want, you have to motivate him. In this case, we needed to prove these leads were worth their time and had value. At least the CEO thought they had value.

I proposed we mail all leads an offer to get our $150 User Manual for free if they would fill out a "Red Sheet". (The User Manual was the best way to evaluate software then.) The Red Sheet was a questionnaire that asked numerous penetrating questions:

- Are you planning to purchase graphics software in the next six months?

- What is your budget?

- What are your main criteria for choosing a graphics software package?

- What competitors are you considering?

These red sheets were gold. We could give our sales reps leads had money to spend, told us how they were going to evaluate the software and who our competition was. The reps called each and every Red Sheet. These were now live potential customers with a budget and intent to purchase in the next six months, not literature collectors. We had solved the follow-up problem by having the customer pre-qualify himself. We didn't need an expensive tracking system that would have forced reps to waste valuable selling time claiming they had made calls.

I have used this technique at four other companies with great success. On the web, it's even easier. Offer something of value that helps the customer make a positive purchase decision in exchange for having the customer qualify himself. One company offers a free live demonstration of their software. They would do this anyway, but the customer views it as even more valuable if he has to earn it.

Don't ignore people calling, writing, or now, clicking to get information from your company. Those are good leads, but you can't expect your reps to diligently pursue every inquiry. So don't make it an exercise for them to qualify leads. That's better done by non-sales people, even the customer himself. Your sales reps need their time to sell, and with qualified leads they'll be eager to do so.

Lastly, you should always know the relative quality of your leads and allocate the best leads to your best reps. Managers often give the best leads to the new or low-performing reps in an effort to level the playing field. No. The new reps should prove they can sell before they earn hot leads. This is motivational because the new reps want to move up and get the best leads, a dangling carrot of sorts, and the successful reps are spurred by their own success.

8. Positivity

Reward, not Punish

When sales reps are not doing what you think they should be

doing, don't punish the violators. Instead, publicly reward those who are doing what you want.

One of the companies I worked with had just instituted a CRM. Two months after it launched, their VC (who got the CRM's reports for reasons I do not know) bellowed that they weren't having enough customer seminars. All hell broke loose. The reps stopped selling and started scheduling customer seminars, or at least reporting they were scheduling them. The next month, the number of seminars shot through the roof and sales plummeted. Now the reps know they have to fake reports that say they're having seminars, just to keep management off their back so they can focus on selling.

Badgering your reps won't improve sales. Positive incentives are far more effective than arbitrary punishments. And reports are only as good as a rep's motivation to actually do what she's reporting. Again, remember: it's easy to get a sales rep to fake call reports; it's hard to motivate a sales rep to make more sales calls.

Have Fun Motivating

Have I mentioned that reps thrive on recognition? An unexpected phone call or email from the CEO is magic, and an award is even better. The beauty of all these motivating tactics is they remind you and your executives to regularly recognize your reps' contributions. They will know they're being noticed. That's vital. But you don't have to stop with sales—recognize achievement throughout your company.

I remember fondly an employee banquet at Instant Supply. I

had a superb partner, my cofounder and CEO, Nick Andrews. I was Chairman. Near the end of the banquet, I asked to speak and presented Nick a plaque, giving him the "CEO of The Year" award. It was sort of a joke, since we only had one CEO, but it gave me an opportunity to recognize his contributions throughout that year. I enjoyed it. He loved it.

One last note: if you hear someone say, "We need to train the sales rep how to do it," translate it into, "We need to motivate the sales rep to do it." Training is easy; motivation is hard. I once attended a presentation by an author named Robert Mager who co-wrote the book *Analyzing Performance Problems*. He had reduced the issue to a simple question: "If his life depended upon it, could an employee do it correctly?" If the answer is "yes", it is a motivation problem not a training problem. He already knows how to do it; he just doesn't want to. Hopefully the tips in this chapter can help you change his mind.

SECTION 5

KEY TAKEAWAYS

CHAPTER 25

The Ten Principles of Sustained Hypergrowth

This chapter is what I hope you take away from my book.

My premise is that growing the number of sales reps plus having a motivational sales comp plan are two of the most important jobs of a CEO. The CEO should understand and approve even a minor change to the sales reps' compensation plan. He should understand, approve and monitor the sales rep hiring plan. And he should internalize these eleven tenets of high sales growth.

The Ten Principles of Sustained Hypergrowth:

1. Sales reps cause sales.

2. Sales reps are free.

3. The job of the sales rep is to bring those resources to bear to cause the sale.

4. The most important job of the sales rep is to retain current customers.

5. New customers are the result of new sales reps in new territories.

6. Compensation plans should be uncapped and encourage the sales rep to invest in his territory long term.

7. Sales reps need a great sales manager on a parallel long-term compensation plan.

8. You should motivate your sales reps with recognized achievement, not policing.

9. The job of each department is to help the sales reps get more orders sooner.

10. If you want to grow your business geometrically, you have to grow your salesforce geometrically.

Follow these tenets and enjoy your hypergrowth.

Chapter 26

Lingering Questions

Prior to publishing, when this book was being reviewed by a few CEOs, VCs, and VP Sales, they all had some great suggestions.

Instead of delaying the publishing date, I decided to address the two most common of their issues in a brief out of place chapter. This is a precursor and complement to our website (www.SalesRepsAreFree.com) that will continue to clarify issues for you.

The Misunderstood Role of Sales Quotas

I hesitate to even mention sales quotas for sales rep because it is so tempting to base compensation on a percentage of quota. That is very wrong and it drives your best reps into your competitor's arms.

Sales quotas do have a valuable role in planning. They should be used as a bottom-up forecasting tool and should be discussed, not negotiated, between your sales reps and your first line sales managers. By taking compensation out of the mix, you can actually get your reps and managers best opinion as to what the potential is for a territory in the coming year. Then, you can maybe do something about the result, like add new reps, new products, or expand into a new geography if the number comes up short.

If you add compensation into the mix, you distort the data. If you pay for a higher forecast, you'll get one. If you pay commission on a percentage of quotas, you'll get very low forecasts. I know, this is so obvious that I am boring you, but, why then is quota the basis for most sales comp plans at stalled companies? If it is so obvious, why do companies do it? I am perplexed. Don't let it happen at your company.

As soon as you add money to the conversation, you get distortion.

Time Frame For Your Sales Comp Plan

We have plans that reset monthly, quarterly, and annually which brought up the time frame questions. I believe in an annual plan from the date of hire for most products and services. But there are exceptions, and these don't preclude the use of daily, weekly, monthly or quarterly accelerators.

The length of your plan depends largely upon the sales cycle. If you're selling magazine subscriptions by phone, you probably have daily and weekly motivators. Try to lock in your great reps, even those selling magazine subscriptions.

One lock-in technique used by ski resorts is to pay minimum wage for lift operators but put $1.00 per hour worked in a fund to be paid if you are still working at the resort on March 31st. Most lift operators are bored and split by then, but the resorts need some of them to stay. After working at minimum wage for three months, they'll stay for the extra month because it is a lump sum of $1,000. For a ski bum that is gold.

At Retail Buying Group and Asia Soft, we have quarterly accelerators with a yearly plan. It works well. At Social Marketing we have weekly accelerators built around an annual plan. At EduCorp, we only have an annual plan due to the long sell cycle.

I would set the accelerators at the frequency of the sales cycle. If it takes 60 days to close, set quarterly accelerators, if one call, weekly ones and so on. I would still put an annual plan in place overall.

CHAPTER 27

Four Books that Are at Least Ten Times Better than this One

These four books changed my business life. They influence how I operate, how I think, and how I do business every day. I consider them "must reads" for any business person. Though I doubt you will, I hope you treasure my book as much as I have treasured these.

1. *Confessions of an Advertising Man*, David Ogilvy

Written by one of my heroes and the founder of Ogilvy Mather Advertising, *Confessions of an Advertising Man* is a business masterpiece. I stumbled onto it one evening while looking to learn how to measure advertising. I found that and much more, including three great "How To" chapters on "How to Write Great Headlines", "How to Write Great Copy" and "How to Write a Great Catalog". Ogilvy's book gave me the push and the confidence to start my first business: Instant Supply Catalog.

You should read his book not only to learn how to write great headlines but to realize there are rules that work in advertising, and those rules can be measured. Catalogs and now web sites particularly enable A vs. B testing, whereby you can test two different approaches and see which is most effective. Just as doubling the size of your sales force can double sales, doubling the effectiveness of your customer communication can double your "hot" leads, which in turn can double revenue.

To further tempt you, here are some of the book's proven rules:

- Long copy sells better than short copy. This is still true on the web as it was in catalogs. Not many people know this, especially art directors.

- You should use one of fifteen specific words in all headlines: New, Free, Announcing...

- Never use Sans Serif typeface (all ad agencies use Sans Serif since they are art based, not sales based).

- And never use white type on a black background.

As a birthday gift from my staff (many birthdays ago), I had the opportunity to spend an evening with Ogilvy at his Chateau in France. At the time, my catalog company was using Ogilvy Direct in London. Spending time with David was one of the great moments of my business career. After reviewing my catalog, which religiously followed all his tenets, David wrote on it, "You are my best student." I have that catalog on my bookshelf today. It is my matchbox car.

2. *Positioning: The Battle for Your Brain,* Al Ries and Jack Trout

I consider this one of the best marketing books ever written, a master treatise on effective branding and the power of branding. Replete with colorful, real-world examples, the book is a delightful read with very powerful concepts. The authors followed it up with *Marketing Warfare* another one of my favorites

Positioning demonstrates that a brand can stand for one—and only one—concept in the mind of the customer. In the first edition from 1981, the authors explain that IBM means computers (it did at the time) and Xerox means copiers, which explains why Xerox couldn't effectively sell computers under the Xerox brand and IBM couldn't sell copiers under the IBM brand. They both tried and failed.

I was so impressed with the concepts of this book I invited Al Ries to speak to the CEOs of all the companies that one of the Valley's venture capital companies funded. I believe he had a real effect on their strategy and helped many achieve greater success.

3. *Coaching for Improved Work Performance,* Ferdinand Fournies

This is the best, most pragmatic people-management book I've ever read. In three days it converted me from a horrible manager to a fairly good one (depending on whom you ask). Fournies, a professor at Columbia Business School, teaches you how to recognize the achievement of your staff every day and how to nudge people to do what the organization needs.

My favorite vignette involved a 51-year-old married man who decided to use Fournies' management techniques to motivate his wife to put the cap back on the toothpaste without her even knowing she was being managed. In the few instances when she did put the cap back on, he dropped everything he was doing, hugged her, and said, "I love you." In a couple of weeks, she was religiously putting the cap on the toothpaste and didn't even know she had been "managed" into doing so.

Good management requires training and practice; you can't expect it to just "come naturally". As Fournies says:

> If I asked you to kneel down and I placed a sword upon your shoulder and said "I dub thee Pilot, go forth and fly an airplane." You would say, "But I don't know how to fly an airplane." Yet, every day in business we have associates kneel down in front of us while we place a sword upon their shoulder and say, "I dub thee manager; go forth and manage." Management is more difficult than flying an airplane.

I had the pleasure of taking Fournies' three-day course before he wrote his book. It was fabulous. And I can attest that the book, like its author, is hilarious.

4. *Analyzing Performance Problems: Or, You Really Oughta Wanna*, Robert F. Mager and Peter Pipe

This, as the title implies, is an analytical management book. It complements Fournies' coaching book quite well.

The key to this diminutive book is the flowchart at the beginning. It quickly enables you to differentiate between a training problem and a motivational problem. As I mentioned in the "Motivators" chapter, Mager and Pipe ask, "Could the employee do the task correctly if his life depended on it?" If the answer is "Yes", then it is not a training problem; it's a motivational problem. Those are much harder to solve, often requiring management skills like those outlined in Fournies' book.

Analyzing Performance Problems is quite clinical and not like the other three books, but it is a key to figuring out performance problems and, better yet, performance solutions.

Years ago, Robert Mager personally helped me with a motivation issue. I attended his two-day course while I was working at Rugged Computer Corp. I mentioned that our Training Manager never set up the training room on Friday before customers arrived on Monday. He would leave at about 4pm on Friday. I'd check the room, find it a disaster, and begrudgingly set it up myself. I was "rewarding non-performance." Mager wisely suggested: "Sit him down. Tell him you are never going to do it again. Tell him it is his responsibility, and then the key is not to do it for him."

At five on the next Friday, as I was departing my office, I glanced at the training room. It was a disaster. It killed me to leave. On Monday morning I came in intentionally late so I'd arrive after the customers. The Training Manager stormed into my office, red faced and screaming. "You didn't set up the training room. Customers are here and it's filthy, and no demo computers are set up." He was ready to slug me. That was the last time I had to mention setting up the room, from then on he did it without me even suggesting it.

Mager and Pipe, better than anyone else I've read, teach you how to motivate people to actually do their jobs.

It worked for me with my four-year old son. He had an electric three-wheeled vehicle that he adored. I told him that after riding it he needed to plug it in so it would be ready to go the next day. I saw it sitting not plugged in and it killed me not to do it for him. But I didn't. My son never missed another day plugging it in. I learned more than he that day.

APPENDIX I

About the Authors

This book is a compilation of learning by three primary authors, who moved up the ladder from selling to marketing to CEOing to founding their own companies. The lessons learned selling and managing sales reps were significant in the success of our companies. Two of the companies went public, and two were sold at a good return to investors. We collaborated with over 10 sales manager and 100's of sales reps. This book aggregates thirty years of experience with these concepts and includes examples from over twenty-plus companies. The concepts hold true for service companies and product companies selling through direct sales reps, catalogs, or the web.

Each chapter and sales story is written in the first person to be more immediate and engaging. The stories are real. The companies are disguised. And the concepts, we believe, are accurate.

After refining the basic tenets of the book, we tested them in depth with five major sales research projects, where we dug deeply into five different companies that were experiencing sales growth stagnation. They ranged from a computer hardware company, to a pure services firm, a retail buying service firm, to an enterprise software company, and finally to a VC/PE firm.

We are proud of the results of these projects: one firm's growth took off from 5% per year to 40%, and they went public nine months after we completed our project. A second company grew from a small software firm with five phone sales reps to an international firm with 192 sales reps worldwide. The third grew 100% in two years, after modest growth the prior two years, and also went public. The VC firm instituted numerous recognitions for their associates that at least made the environment better, and the final project is too soon to tell.

We think we have some good ideas that can help businesses grow more rapidly. That helps society many ways: companies grow creating more employment and wealth around the world, more people and companies get great products and services; shareholders get higher returns so they will invest in more companies; and much to our delight, more sales reps get hired, which in turn drives employment in all departments of the company.

We hope we've helped.

Bill Conifer

Bill Conifer

Appendix II

Glossary Of Companies

AdSalesCo. – This was a pure internet ad sales organization selling foreign and remnant banner ads on major internet sites. It had a highly motivational sales compensation plan, and had an aggressive sales rep hiring program. It worked well.

AsiaSoft – a pure software company that markets to major companies and governments worldwide. Stalled growth with five sales reps at the time of our involvement. Five years later, they have over 190 sales reps worldwide, with revenue growth of over 30% per year.

ATM Cash – this is a company that placed ATMs into businesses locations. It had seven sales reps and, at the time of our involvement, the CEO had just introduced a sales compensation plan that would have forced all their sales reps to join their competitor. The sales plan was revised to encourage long term contracts and two years later with 80% of ATM's customers on long term, auto-renew, contracts, their competitors had nowhere to sell.

Buying Group – this is a service company that provides buying services to small medical offices. By grouping their purchases, the Buying Group can deliver high discounts to small offices with little purchasing power. At the time of our analysis, they had five sales reps, which following our proposed plan have been expanded to 15 reps. After stalled growth, they have doubled the number of new customers this year over last year, accelerating growth to 30%.

EduCorp. – Computer hardware company targeting elementary education. At the time of our engagement the company was had stalled growth with seven sales reps. Upon following our recommendations for a new compensation plan and an expanded sales force, growth took off, exceeding over 50% per year for the next two years, at which time they were acquired.

Graphics Soft – an enterprise level graphics software package sold to research departments of universities and corporations. It grew rapidly and then leveled off. Our analysis was that they stopped growing because they stopped hiring at five sales reps. We could not convince them to hire more. They did supplement the external reps with internal reps. The focus was to make the five more successful. It worked marginally and the company was sold.

Instant Supply – a business to business catalog targeting the computer industry. It is a good way to see the value of adding selling power.

Minicomputer Corp. - One of many minicomputer companies that pre dated the personal computer boom. They sold almost exclusively to businesses. Numerous examples are used from this experience since the data was so clear. Hire a sales rep this year and he or she will produce $1,000,000 in revenue next year.

Office Soft Corp. – one of many software companies selling through the big box office retailers to small and medium businesses. These examples enable us to demonstrate using a retail store shelf as a sales rep. The key to these businesses is number of stores times the number of products per store. Like Instant Supply, it makes a good parallel example of hiring more sales reps with a simple compensation plan.

Palo Alto Electronics – this is an electronic instrument company that had an appreciation of hiring a lot of sales reps but with a damaged and de-motivational sales commission plan. They grew at a 10 to 20% rate due to sales rep hiring. With a motivation compensation plan this company could have had rapid growth.

Rugged Computer Corp. – this is a company that marketed computers to the military. It again had five sales reps but succeeded due to the fact that selling a computer into a government program can breed a very large volume of sales if the program goes to production. One did. They could have been much bigger if they had expanded the sales force, especially to Europe.

Social Marketing – this is a service company that provided small retailers with social media marketing help. They would offer programs that drove traffic into retailers, and monitored their Yelp and Google reviews. At the time of our engagement, they had seven internal sales reps in one location. We recommended a distributed sales organization. The first month of our new remote sales office, the new office exceeded the revenue of the corporate sales office, doubling their business.

Made in the USA
Middletown, DE
16 January 2016